Hearts of Flesh

Fred Pruitt

1663 LIBERTY DRIVE, SUITE 200
BLOOMINGTON, INDIANA 47403
(800) 839-8640
WWW.AUTHORHOUSE.COM

First published by AuthorHouse 04/29/05

ISBN: 1-4208-4247-1 (sc)

Printed in the United States of America
Bloomington, Indiana

This book is printed on acid-free paper.

To Bob Beeland
The first Christ-face I saw when I started to wake up

All scripture quotations are from the King James Bible of 1611.

Cover Art: Michael Hillman
Cover Design: Steve Eilers

Table of Contents

Introduction

What is contained in the following pages is not a systematic presentation of Christian religious principles or teaching. We have our basis there, but from that foundation we move into what is for many the rest and peace of God, which we find when we experience the Living God as our "personal" inner Life. This is what we discover when we consciously move into living in union with God as the source of, and everyday moment-by-moment sustenance of, our own self and everything else of life.

This book has been written from a perspective of life in Jesus Christ, but anyone, regardless of confession, may find something joyously familiar here, because "Christ in us" is a universal truth, and may be known by any of us in everything that is.

That truth is this: *"The mystery which hath been hid from ages and from generations, but now is made manifest to his saints … which is Christ in you, the hope of glory."*[1]

There are no principles presented here to memorize and start practicing. There are no instructions whatsoever except one: to believe God.

I read a story a long time ago about a man who was walking somewhere in a light mist, so light that it was almost unnoticeable and he gave it no mind. When he got to where he was going, he realized he had become soaking wet.

That is what the kingdom of God is like.

May you look and find yourself soaking wet as well.

Hearts of Flesh

Someone once said that the first time his son's toy truck broke he realized that his son was beginning his acquaintance with the Man of Sorrows. It made him want to tear his heart out, but at the same time he knew it had to be, and that the end result would one day be overwhelming joy.

Paul said that the sign of Christ in us, rather than the rote keeping of the Law, is that we would have hearts of flesh, instead of hearts of stone.[2]

A heart of flesh has known what it means to have no hope. It has wallowed in its aloneness and fear of the dark. It knows disappointment, failure and barrenness, and more than once perhaps has wished it could die and be no more.

But this heart has also found light in the furthest parts of darkness, unexpectedly, seemingly undeserved, but nonetheless certain, solid and perceptible in the substance of faith. In its rising the heat of that light melts the cold stone of our hearts, changing them to soft, innocent, guile-free hearts of warm, loving flesh.

Then -- we have become flesh instead of stone, and our hearts, through joy and sorrow, have been penetrated through and through with love that spills out of us like water.

The Secret Name

I have this misty image that is always with me. I am a young child, and I have a fever. In the delirium of the fever, when consciousness is swirling between dream, sleep, and wakefulness, I hear a voice that seems to come from a distance, from an unseen and unperceived source. It comes from somewhere beyond the swirl in my mind. I'm only vaguely conscious of the swirl, since I am caught up in the fever and simply living in it without will, being carried along on its waves.

The voice seems the most familiar voice in all the world; and it's a loving voice, comforting, soothing me in my fevered confusion. Though not quite asleep, not quite awake and not quite aware, still in that dimness I can hear the voice saying only one thing -- my name.

"Fred… Fred… Fred."

Finally I am aware enough to know that it's my mother, speaking only my name. I can only barely comprehend who she is, but it doesn't matter that my mind can't grasp the fullness of who she is, because her voice is enough, just saying my name, and by her voice she sends peace into my fever

...

That image has stayed with me all these years, and more and more it has grown in me that God speaks in us in this way. He speaks out of a mist, out of the unknown, out of the unfamiliar, as a distinct voice and within all the other voices.

From Him we hear our "secret name" that no one else can hear. Each of us, in the center of our own existence, where no one else can be, is intimately alone with God. And the reason hearing our Name is secret is because He speaks our Name in the secret place, where only He and I are, and we cannot speak of that place, nor describe it.

When we hear Him, He is calling our names from out of the mist of the confusion and chaos of the world. When He says our names, He speaks our individual lives into existence.

"Samuel, Samuel!"

"Speak, Lord, thy servant heareth."[3]

He has spoken each of our names from eternity. He has seen each of us in His mind and heart and desired to live in the midst of everything that we are, by walking in us and being our God.[4] And so with the force of a billion-megaton atomic bomb, in a rushing heat of eternal Divine desire, His Love spun the universe out of His Word. He did it so that He could fulfill His own pleasure, by being the fire in our inward parts, the light in our minds, and the love that comes out of our deepest center.

Adequacy

On a just-turning crisp fall day in 1980, leaves starting to fall, my wife Janis and I took a forty-five minute road trip through the north Georgia countryside to Kennesaw, where we were going to have what we thought would be a "counseling session" with an "old missionary," Norman Grubb.

I was used to having a "minister" tell you what to think do, to interpret God's will for you. We had more or less been programmed to think that way. But now we were coming to Norman to hopefully unravel the knot we were tied in. I knew he was a famous missionary and author and I hoped he could help us find God's will again and get back on track. We had recently left a ministry we'd been involved with for seven years, something we felt we'd had no choice but to do, but still we were eaten up with guilt and condemnation for all kinds of good reasons.

When we got there I started in on my tirade, my justifications, my heart desires to "only please the Lord," all the wrongs done us, etc., etc., etc. Blah blah blah blah.

At some point in my presentation I said something about needing ministers "above" me to show me God's way (always trying to prove my humility). It was like a bolt of lightning hit eighty-five year old Norman. Up until that time he'd been slumped over against one side of a wingback chair, looking disinterested and half asleep. But when I said that about "needing ministers," he suddenly straightened up like he was hit with fifty thousand volts! Then he raised one finger and fervently told me that I didn't need "any man" to teach me, that <u>Christ was already my total adequacy and teacher inside me</u>!

I don't remember the exact words he said, or anything else he said in that meeting for that matter. I just remember that bells, whistles and foghorns went off, lights flashed, birds sang, every valley was filled and all mountains became plains in that one double-whammy instant of realization. Scales fell from my eyes; frozen rivers suddenly cracked and ice began to break up; flowers broke through the barren topsoil, and the abundance of lush summer green popped out of every fiber of the fabric of creation.

All the issues I'd gone there to get answers for -- What should I do about this, What should I think about that? What about the people left behind? What about their teaching? Did I do right? Did I do wrong? Was it God's will? Am I in God's will? All those questions and their hundreds of already-speculated answers went flying out the window into the land of irrelevancy.

In a moment, eternity opened up and I saw the whole ball of wax.

God -- Father, Son, Holy Spirit -- IS my permanent indwelling adequacy!

Simple, right? Surely someone had mentioned that before. I had been part of a Charismatic/Pentecostal church, which believed in the infilling of the Spirit and all the gifts. So I surely believed in the Holy Spirit living in me. Even had the "gifts" working, which should have been fair evidence to my mind.

But this was something different. Despite my charismatic training about being "filled with the Spirit," which I had experienced numerous times, I still lived in my mind apart from God and was self-condemned most of the time. Since God was still apart from me in my consciousness, the infilling of the Spirit seemed to come

Remind 6-7-8 pages

from outside me and <u>was directly dependent (I thought)</u> <u>upon my performance, behavior, habits, and self-discipline.</u> (Which I always found lacking in myself.)

And so, even though knowing the "indwelling of the Spirit," and practicing the use of the "gifts" for years, still I had no inkling of the permanent adequacy of God within me, and even less of an inkling that in "receiving Him," He had become one person with me.[5]

The issue on the line that day, every day before, and <u>every day since, is this: Is the inner adequacy of Christ</u> <u>steadfast</u> every moment on its own, with no help from <u>"me"</u> (i.e. "my" efforts)?" <u>Is God really</u> a well of water springing up into everlasting life, Who will cause me to never thirst again?[6] Is the water always there, springing up to overflowing?

<u>That day, I saw in a heartbeat that it was true.</u> A shift in <u>my consciousness began in earnest that day, starting with</u> <u>knowing God's adequacy as permanently residing in me, to</u> <u>the even further "knowing" of Christ living in me as simply</u> <u>my regular "me," instead of some stylized idyllic image I</u> <u>had conjured up in my head which never appeared.</u> like better

And everyday that same question rears its head, and every day the answer is the same. The question always is this: Is God sufficient, right now, in me, in this present moment? The answer is always: YES! Have I died in His death and been raised again to new life, so that He is now <u>joined with me as one spirit, one person, within me?</u> In <u>other words, is Christ my True Real Self?</u>

Other questions are irrelevant here. No other questions belong here. Questions like: "Well, if it was Christ living in me, then why is my life like this? If Christ is living my life, then how come this happened, or that?"

All those questions are answered by answering the One Primary Question: Who are you?[7] First things first. *"Seek ye first the kingdom."*

The answer we give is a present moment answer because God is only in the present moment. We will not discover Him in the past or the future. God only lives in reality, and past and future are not real. All that is real is right now.

And today is the day of salvation. Today is the day the Holy Spirit speaks. Today, *"Thou are my son, this day I have begotten thee."*[8]

The day is eternal now. This day God has begotten you as His son. Don't worry about yesterday, or tomorrow. Today is the Day of God. And today He has begotten you as His son. Today, right now, is the moment of faith.

"No, wait a minute, I was saved on June 5th, 1958, and...."

No, no, no -- you miss my point. Yes, maybe there was an earth day, the "day" you were saved, the day you finally turned to the Lord with all your heart. O Glory Day! Hallelujah!

But every day is the day of salvation! Every day He is begetting us anew even as the Son is always new, fresh, and innocent.

The reason is that God bursts out of the Eternal by His Love and takes up dwelling in time in us through the power of His own desire. His Love is the instigator and the empowerment, not something coming from us. Every moment is His moment, every situation His situation, every obstacle His obstacle, every negative His purposed negative.

7

i.e.
more
than
sufficient
in
Him
note

Why? Because he puts us to the test, not to test "us" to prove that we are inadequate, but to ~~prove~~ Show Himself in us. He overcomes all things. It is a purifying ordeal, trial by fire, but it is not to find all the bad stuff in us and make us give it up. All that is gone in changing kingdoms from darkness to light. The only "bad stuff" in us was the wicked one, who had secretly hidden himself spiritually in our false independence, and now in the Cross and death of Jesus and our death in Him and with Him, the wicked one is cast out of us, and in the resurrection we rise in Him as servants of righteousness only.

The "trial of faith" is therefore to make our faith as pure gold. And our faith as pure gold is simply this: that we latch in our consciousness onto one faith "object," and one only, the Living God. God purifying our faith then means His further and further solidifying our faith capacity onto God Only, and nothing else -- no other person or persons, no church, no teaching, no books, no possessions, no social position, nothing else except God Himself as we each know Him in the inner depths and foundation of our being.

In other words, just nekkid God and nekkid you. Everything else stripped away.

"*Thou shalt have no other gods before me.*"[9] That's the very first commandment.

He sees to it. You don't have to. Anything you do to try to look good and attract God's attention to how much you dedicate yourself to Him is laughable vanity. I know. You can't consecrate enough. There's always more to do and become because He is above all we ask or think and we can never do, know, or be enough to reach Him.

Likewise you can't mess up enough to get Him off your back, either. You can try to *"believe not,"* but He *"abides faithful."*[10]

In hell, when you can't speak because of your thirst, when you can't believe because it's just too preposterous, when you can't take another step because it's pointless, when victory is not possible because you have not worked hard enough or said the right words or made the right incantations, when everything seems lost and it seems you made a wrong turn somewhere and got hopelessly lost out in the boondocks -- is Christ right then and there your total adequacy and are you One with Him?

Do you say YES?

It's easy to believe when all is hunky-dory.

A storm suddenly bearing down on us in the middle of the sea can change all that in a heartbeat. We quake with fear, and know surely we've done something wrong, or there wouldn't be a storm.

Right then and there in the midst of the storm, ourselves cowering in fear in this fragile little boat, a Man who'd gone unnoticed for a while, forgotten, asleep in the back of the boat, arises and with no effort speaks and stops the wind and the sea.

That Man is You and I. He has risen in our lives and wears our identities now as his. And He is our permanent inner Adequacy, our hidden True Self.[11] In the incarnation Christ is formed in you and me.[12]

Isaiah 60

1 Arise, shine; for thy light is come, and the glory of the LORD is risen upon thee.

2 For, behold, the darkness shall cover the earth, and gross darkness the people: but the LORD shall arise upon thee, and his glory shall be seen upon thee.

3 And the Gentiles shall come to thy light, and kings to the brightness of thy rising.

You do understand, don't you, that the Messiah dwells in you, and this passage, which refers to Him, describes you?

A Little Word on Faith

Faith, like everything else, is not of ourselves.

Faith is the word of God welling up in the inward parts of our being.

It comes, not at our own whim, but at the precise point where it is necessary.

It comes in despair, when we cannot take another step.

It comes when death seems imminent, and it testifies of life, which cannot yet be seen.

It comes rising up as a Living Word, from beyond ourselves as if out of nowhere, and lifts us up on our feet.

When we don't know the way, when we can't see the path, when doubt seems the order of the day, every moment faith says, "This is the way, walk ye in it".... "Just take the next step"....

Faith is being billowed over by Him Who is invisible -- imperceptible, utterly Beyond -- and yet more familiar than our own skin.

Faith is being carried along in the midst of our doubt in the river that waters everything in abundance.

Regardless of how the deck looks stacked; regardless of the utter impossibility of a child being born to a dead womb; regardless of the fact that no lepers have ever been cleansed before, regardless of the fact that no one born blind has ever been made to see, faith continues to say that things we cannot see are real and true.

By faith, blind eyes see, lepers are cleansed; and children are born which could not have been born.

Faith is rest -- once the battle has been settled -- rest in God accomplishing what He said He would accomplish.

Faith is saying to God, as did the mother of our Lord, *"Be it unto me according to thy word."*[13]

In saying that, Mary acknowledged that it was God Who would accomplish this great thing, the Christ being born of her. In the same way, we say to God, *"Be it unto me according to thy word."*

"Let Christ be born in me!" Not by my might, my intellect, my good looks, my dedication, my spirituality, not by anything of "me," but by thy Spirit!

Faith says it is so. What He has said He would do, He has done -- *"I will dwell in them and walk in them, and be their God."*[14]

Though the world rages against it, though even our own psyche rebels and says it couldn't possibly be so, nevertheless faith rises up and says, "God Himself is the doer of all in me!"

Faith is the foretaste of the heavenly country. It is the actual substance[15] of the things we see afar off and hope for. It is the solid conclusive evidence of Him Who is unseen, unheard, unknown by the world, but revealed in the depths of our spirits.

Therefore, as Paul said, let us lift up our weak knees, and hear the word of faith shouting deep in our hearts. And that word is this:

Looking not unto ourselves, but unto Him, we are confident of this very thing, that he which hath begun a good work in you will perform it until the day of Jesus Christ."[16]

Abraham

Abraham in old age, childless, receives a vision from God telling him he's going to have an heir, a "seed" which shall bless all nations. *"And he believed in the LORD; and he counted it to him for righteousness."*[17]

But years go by and Abraham and Sarah are getting older, past childbearing age, and the "vision" Abraham received hasn't come true yet, so she suggests Abraham "go in unto" her Egyptian maid, Hagar. Which Abraham promptly does, not having to be told twice. Hagar conceives, and the child born is called Ishmael.

Twelve years later the promise is fulfilled when ninety year old Sarah conceives and bears Isaac, the "son of promise."

Later Hagar and Sarah aren't getting along, so Sarah wants Hagar and Ishmael sent away, since Ishmael is a potential threat to her son's inheritance. This causes Abraham a crisis, but God speaks to him again and tells him to go along with his wife on this, that He has a plan for Ishmael, too -- he'll be the father of twelve kings -- but the fullness of His promise rests with Isaac. So Abraham sends Hagar and his son Ishmael away, and they almost perish in the desert, but are rescued by angels.

It is easy to read that story and to judge Abraham guilty of weaknesses or failures in the flesh. His "listening to his wife" and his liaison with Hagar are often taught as Abraham's fleshly attempt to bring about the promise by a descent into sin. Many of us have been snagged in the fear that we seek to bear the children of the flesh, and we are convinced that all the apparent ghastly failures we've suffered have been precisely because of our adulterous affairs with the flesh. For some of us everything is "always our fault."

A good case can be made for that with Abraham. I mean, look at the mess we're in now. Who are the Arabs? Ishmaelites! The Arabs especially, and all Muslims indirectly, take their lineage from Abraham via Ishmael.

And look at the prophecy from Genesis regarding Ishmael and his descendants: *"And he will be a wild man; his hand will be against every man, and every man's hand against him; and he shall dwell in the presence of all his brethren."*[18]

That was written several thousand years ago about the descendants of Ishmael -- that should give anyone pause.

So it seems therefore, given all the current trouble stirred up by the Ishmaelites, that we can certainly make a case for Abraham having left the plan of God momentarily when he "listened to his wife."

I think not.

First of all, how do we convict Abraham of sin? What he did was normal for his time. There was no law against it, nor was it in the least uncommon for a wealthy man, as Abraham was, to have the pleasure of more than one wife or concubines. The Lord did not once rebuke him for it, nor did his legal affair with Hagar affect in any way the fulfillment of God's Promise.

It was simply Abraham living his life. When Abraham "believed in the Lord, and he counted it as righteousness," Abraham was sealed in the kingdom of God. He was God's man, through and through. He has God's heart, God's mind, and God's desires, implanted in the depths of his being. He walked God's walk, talked God's talk. His entire life was the sanctity of Christ.

When God told him everywhere he put his foot was his land, God wasn't really talking about real estate. It was the same as that which Samuel told Saul, *"And let it be, when these signs are come unto thee, that thou do as occasion serve thee; for God is with thee."*[19] In other words, live your life, and that IS God. Why? Because you have learned all the concepts, precepts, rules and requirements and are now able to walk by them? No, it is because His Spirit dwells in us to will and to do the works of God!

Abraham was a New Testament man. To have been "counted righteous" by the Lord, means more than a legal pronouncement, but a living empowerment from Christ within, who is living righteousness. And God is the God of truth and reality so that when He "counts," He counts with absolute truth and honesty. His "counted righteousness" must therefore be an actual righteousness, and not a make-believe-because-I-said-it kind.

What I'm saying is there was no sin in Abraham going in unto Hagar and fathering Ishmael, despite the mess we have today. It was, and IS, God's plan. Including the mess. Abraham didn't sin. (If he did where is the rebuke of God for it? What man will condemn Abraham if there is no record of God having done so?) He walked in His Father's Righteousness.

Did he and Sarah mistakenly think that their little scheme would help along the plan of God? Maybe. It doesn't matter what they thought. Abraham believed in the Lord, and the Lord counted it as righteousness. Abraham put every day in the hands of God. That's enough to walk in the Spirit, which is to be Christ living as us expressed in our frail human selves, despite the thoughts and fears that go through our minds.

15

My point is this. Union -- unity -- with God, means just that living today and tomorrow is Christ living in us but hidden in normal weak-looking human living -- reactions and decisions and emotions and actions and whatever else we do or see or hear or think.

We are in His Kingdom, and therefore all things are pure. Have at it. All of you, spirit, soul and body, is pure. Go for it.

And there is no caveat for that. No further explanatory statement, no warning, no reminder of what to remember if you are part of His Kingdom, but only a trust in nothing but God and no other. The free, "wide impregnable country" of Christ.

Purity is contagious. Once you see it anywhere, it crops up everywhere, and spreads from heart to heart.

A Quick Abrahamic Bible Study

5 And he brought him forth abroad, and said, Look now toward heaven, and tell the stars, if thou be able to number them: and he said unto him, So shall thy seed be.

6 And he believed in the LORD; and he counted it to him for righteousness.[20]

16 Now to Abraham and his seed were the promises made. He saith not, And to seeds, as of many; but as of one, And to thy seed, which is Christ.[21]

If the "Seed" of Abraham is Christ, and God said in His promise to Abraham, pointing to the innumerable stars in the heavens and saying, *"So shall thy seed be,"* then God, in His promise, was making reference to an innumerable company, and that company, the City of God, corporately is Christ, which is Jesus -- and you and me in Him.

What do we think he saw when God showed him the stars of heaven and said, "so shall thy seed be"? Jesus tells us, *"Abraham rejoiced to see my day."*[22] Abraham was a man of the Spirit, who knew the promise of God was not limited merely to his son Isaac and his fleshly descendents, but Abraham saw and embraced the kingdom of God; he foreknew and foresaw the Christ of God.

God opened Abraham's vision to more than physical stars, to more than the fruit of his loins, but to the heavenly promise of redemption in Christ, and the resurrection of the whole world, the entire cosmos, to newness of life. As the *"heavens declare the glory of God and the firmament showeth His handiwork,"*[23] Abraham saw in his vision of God the shining forth of the sons of God, ONE NEW

MAN, as Paul said, which is Christ, All in all, i.e. the "seed" of God.

He had already discovered the *"secret hid from ages and generations,"*[24] in Gen 15:1, *"After these things the word of the LORD came unto Abram in a vision, saying, Fear not, Abram: I am thy shield, and thy exceeding great reward."* This is not some promise of gold or silver, big flocks and fruitful wives, nor even the promise of eternal "rewards" in the hereafter, but of one "thing" only, the Person of God. *"I AM THY SHIELD, AND THY EXCEEDING GREAT REWARD."*

God is saying, "I, Myself, am your reward, Abraham. Your reward is MY SELF living in you!"

Yet Abraham immediately asks God for an heir -- why?[25] If God was his reward, sufficiency and totality, why then did Abraham immediately tell him he felt deficient without an heir? That almost seems ungrateful.

Because this is already the Father's life stirring in him. God's Life exists in us to procreate. It is the basic primal urge of the physical human race (and everywhere I go I see no shortage of babies) to *"be fruitful and multiply and replenish the earth"* (the one commandment in which our race has excelled). If that is the most basic urge of the physical race, how much more does that desire drive the "race from heaven"?

How much more does the Second Adam wish to reproduce Himself? The love drive in the physical, that makes men and women get together, marry, have children and establish a family, is only a shadow compared to the love drive in the Spirit, which binds all in the outflowing love of God, and seeks continuously only to increase love by giving birth to love in others, through the revelation of Christ in each of us.

It was God's stirring in Abraham to ask for an heir, because it was God's plan all along. Abraham was not being faithless or forgetting what had just been revealed to him about God as his All in all. Instead he was expressing through his natural desires for a child of his own body, the equally natural desires of the Heavenly Father for a child of His own body, the fruit of His Own Loins to come forth, which was His Seed, sown in every human created and who breathed God's breath.

Do we see the implications of this? Abraham's NATURAL desire to be a father, to have an heir, mirrored the Love drive in God to see His Son be birthed. The implication I am referring to is the same echo in our own lives. Those same divine stirrings are in our depths, too, hidden in the everyday things of life.

"And he believed in the LORD; and he counted it to him for righteousness." Another of Paul's proof texts, so we say, of the doctrine of justification by faith.

But this is more than a proof text. This is the way things work at the foundation of the universe.

This is more than a mental belief that there is a God, or there is a Christ, or that Jesus is the Savior. It's more than picking a new boss to work for. It's more than changing one's party loyalties.

God has just spoken a great word to him -- *"I am thy exceeding great reward"* -- and shown him a vision of Christ in the stars of heaven and made him a personal promise that those stars represent "his seed" Who is/are to come.

Abraham's "belief" is his losing his life. He has been shifted in his consciousness from his limited perception of himself and the division of this world, to the All Sufficiency of the Living God, seen in the Eternal. God spoke and in his willing reception of the Living Word of God, the Spirit of God filled Abraham in his inner being and became his righteousness. Abraham knew his righteousness, and like others before him and innumerable ones since, knew that even though he walked the earth as normal human "patriarch" Abraham, he lived in and trusted in the Unseen One, and that the life he lived dwelling in tents in Canaan was the life of the Son of God, the Righteousness of God.

We, the Seed of God, the ONE MAN, which is the Christ of God, are subjected to vanity, not of our own will, but by the will of him who subjected us to it.[26] We are subjected to the subtle pulls, side-trips and distractions from the one who would make us believe, if we would, that "vanity" is all there is, like the "preacher" in Ecclesiastes.

He makes a good case, and there are often days upon days when it seems like he's right. We feel alone and forgotten of God and everybody else. The "promise" we heard on the mountain of transfiguration has faded into a pipe dream, a mockery, and the constant accusation of, "You're crazy to believe all that stuff," seems like a respite and certainly more logical and easier to "believe," than some unheard "word" from an invisible God.

It's an old trick, and the deceiver doesn't really seem to know any more tricks than just that one. But as the Father has sent us into vanity to prove <u>Himself,</u> and by means of that vanity to bring many sons to glory, even so faith arises of itself. By nothing we do faith rises at the bottom of the pit of hell/redemption. Like the four lepers, we arise and say, *"Why sit we here til we die?"*[27] We gingerly venture out and find the enemy decimated and the Living God has invisibly won the day.

The bottom line is this, just as it was for Abraham.

"And Abraham believed in the Lord, and it was counted unto him as righteousness."

Again, this is not a proof text. This is reality. To believe in the Lord is to believe in nothing but the Lord. There is nothing else. HE IS the ALL from Whom all things have come, and He has created all out of His Word, His Logos, and fills all that He has created. To "believe in the Lord" is to see Him as the sufficiency, substance and source out of which all things are and in which all things are upheld.

ALL THINGS! We might conclude the term "all things" must literally mean "all things. That would include "all things" -- there is NOTHING that is left out.

People say we blaspheme by believing that, that God fills everything everywhere with nothing but Himself. That it is somehow pantheism or new age or something similar. First Corinthians 15 says the completion is God being All in all, and by grace through faith that completion is fulfilled in us right now. We cannot deny what has plainly been revealed in the depths of our hearts and also in the Scriptures.

Those who are in Christ and have lost their lives in Him already know it, regardless of what doctrines they hold, because to fall into the arms of the Living God, no matter what are our conceptual understandings, is beyond our mental state, and in the realm of the spirit, where true faith is known and exercised above, beyond and through our intellect. Whatever our outer mind may or may not comprehend, inwardly where Spirit is joined with spirit we "know." And that is where faith comes from.

You are the ground, and the seed is Christ. You didn't sow yourself, God did. His seed is stronger than anything in the universe, since it is "of" His seed that the universe consists. It has a life of its own. It grows up of itself, in its own way, in its own time. A little at a time, to our viewpoint. But the day comes, despite the mockers, the judgers, the scoffers, (who we hear in our own head or those out in the world), despite our own self-doubts and thinking the day of the Lord will never come and we've believed in a fairytale; nonetheless the day comes when we see the full corn in the ear.

This garden grows, and it produces, because the husbandman is the Father, not we ourselves. We are only the ground where the seed is cast, but what a great tree comes forth from such a little, insignificant, almost invisible seed, so great a tree that the fowls of the air have their nests in it, and the beasts of the field take cover from the heat of the sun. We are the "tree planted by the rivers of water"[28] that shall never be moved.

Isaac is born, and we look to the stars of heaven and hear the same word Abraham heard, *So shall thy seed be.*

Jesus Christ Is Come In the Flesh

Hereby know ye the Spirit of God:
Every spirit that confesseth that Jesus Christ is come in the
flesh is of God: And every spirit that confesseth not that Jesus
Christ is come in the flesh is not of God: and this is that spirit
of antichrist, whereof ye have heard that it should come; and
even now already is it in the world.[29]

What gravity there is in these verses. Why would such importance be placed on confessing, "*Jesus Christ is come in the flesh*"? Because God taking the form of and manifesting Himself as man is the means whereby He accomplishes His plan to give birth to an eternal family of sons who express His love.

"*How precious also are thy thoughts unto me, O God!*
how great is the sum of them!"[30] Do we realize that God's "thoughts" are the fuel for our "reality"? God's eternal thoughts have created the substance of the reality we are living at this moment.

Our human idea of thought is a sort of inner banter in the mind, but God's thoughts take form and become real. Our own thoughts about ourselves are often self-accusatory, but not so God's! His thoughts (which are "real") are "*precious*" concerning us and "*great is the sum of them.*" More than the number of the sand! For each of us! Can we imagine such a thing?

"*Thine eyes did see my substance, yet being unperfect; and*
in thy book all my members were written, which in continuance
were fashioned, when as yet there was none of them."[31]

When God "thought" of me -- lo, I was created!

23

Of what was I created? Of His Word – *"and He is before all things, and by Him all things consist"*[32].

Created and predestined before the foundation of the earth to walk in Him as His sons, we have been given the privileged gift of self-consciousness and will. "Will" is in the heart of God, because as a Free Person He has with intent fixed Himself in love, and therefore as created selves who reflect Him we have been given the serious, but ultimately joyous inheritance of Freedom, which implies will. Free out of the freedom of God to be who we desire and choose to be! *gift of freedom is from The Love of God for us*

In the Gospel stories nearly everyone had divided loyalties except the Messiah. He stuck to the truth, which was that HE had come in the flesh. *"This day is this scripture fulfilled in your ears."* The Day of the Lord has come -- I Am HE!!!! What chutzpah! What ego!

Yet they nailed Him to a Cross, <u>because</u> they would not believe that God had come in the flesh. They didn't really believe in God. They only believed in their "idea" of God, and that idea could never come in the flesh, because it was only their idea, and not the True God. They were stirred by their harsh taskmaster, the serpent from the beginning, the king of "me for me," who himself would not go in to the Kingdom, and desired to prevent others as well. They had to kill God coming in the flesh because He testified that their god (themselves and the serpent in them) was not true.

"And I heard a great voice out of heaven saying, Behold, the tabernacle of God is with men, and he will dwell with them, and they shall be his people, and God himself shall be with them, and be their God."[33].

Behold, the tabernacle of God is with men -- what can this mean? It is God dwelling in man as the final consummation of creation. It is the purpose of all His "thoughts" toward us, *"Great is the sum of them"* -- *"His tabernacle is with men."*

This is not the tabernacle of the Sinai desert, where everything is hidden, apart and unavailable. No, this tabernacle is God dwelling full-bore with men. God "knowing" (mixing with) man, God manifesting His Eternal Word, His Eternal Son, by means of His created, adopted sons -- Mankind. This is God Himself being the hidden self in Man, redeemed man, THE "Man from heaven," in the many "men from heaven."

Paul calls Jesus, *"the Second Man, the Lord from heaven."*[34] The "Second Man" is eternal "Man," and Jesus is the Lord and King of a new race of eternal "men," who in Him are also the "Second Man," and therefore all corporately the "Lord from heaven." We were all Adam. We are now all the Second Man, the Lord from heaven: Christ.

But that could not happen had not *"Jesus Christ come in the flesh."*

For us, *"this day this scripture is fulfilled in your ears,"* means that Jesus Christ has come now in MY flesh.

The saying today is "outside the box." Saying Christ has now, right now, come in MY flesh, breaks that box to pieces. There is no box to be out of. This is the most ultimate boldness there can be, coupled with the greatest possibility of failure. And that failure is backed up by lots of evidence of bones broken and shattered on the rocks all around this mountain. But this is faith that pulls out all the stops and bets the whole farm and everybody that works on it on Red 23 (God) and then lets the roulette table turn, hoping against hope and against all odds and all histories, that the ball will come to a stop in Red 23. The Pharisees (outside you and inside you) will say that is blasphemy, that God cannot come in flesh, and certainly not in YOUR flesh. "You're crazy and monumentally presumptuous to think Red 23 will come up." Anybody could point out a million reasons why it could not possibly be and why you're such a fool to think it.

But He does come in flesh, and every spirit that confesses that Jesus Christ is come in the flesh is of God. Jesus Christ has come in the flesh so that we may say, "Yes, I have found myself to be in Him, and therefore my flesh, my humanity, is the Carrier of the Divine. He has come, emptied Himself of His divinity, and donned the likeness of my individual humanity, so that my life in this world is the Treasure of Him walking around being my human me. My little individual human existence IS Jesus Christ come in the flesh!"

There is no Christ except He has come in the flesh. Unless He is the Son of Man (as well as the Son of God) He has no meaning to us creatures of flesh. What else can *"I live, yet not I, but Christ liveth in me, and the life I now live in the flesh,"*[35] mean, but that Christ has now come in my flesh?

And this means now. There is nothing to hold us back from saying God is manifest in MY flesh now. There are no deeper understandings we need, no levels to attain, no need to wait til we get a new body to be who we are, or even a need to get "more sanctified" or "closer to God." Today is the day. Right now. God is manifest in MY flesh right now. Spirit, soul and body. IN this particular earthen vessel He shines as a Treasure[36] to those with eyes that see and ears that hear.

Now, today, is this scripture fulfilled in your ears:

"The spirit of the Lord God is upon me; because the Lord hath anointed me to preach good tidings unto the meek; he hath sent me to bind up the brokenhearted, to proclaim liberty to the captives, and the opening of the prison to them that are bound; To proclaim the acceptable year of the LORD."[37]

It is fulfilled today in you and me.

HE has done it.

"This is the Lord's doing, and it is marvelous in our eyes."[38]

Already Are

When we say we are "complete and perfect in Christ," we are not meaning that there is no spiritual "growth" or changes brought into our outer living by the Spirit of Christ who lives in us.

Of course God continues to change and mold us as every day passes. The scripture says, *"But we all, with open face beholding as in a glass the glory of the Lord, are changed into the same image from glory to glory, even as by the Spirit of the Lord."*[39]

The completion I refer to, the "Already are-ness," is He Himself. In Him, I am. But I don't find myself by looking for myself (or for change or "growth" in myself), but by losing myself and finding Him. Then in finding and seeing only Him, I am changed into the same image from glory to glory, plateau to plateau, height to height, peak to peak, by the Spirit of the Lord.

And by simple faith we declare, "O Lord, you have become One with me so that my self is YOU being yourself," and we are thus privileged to see our hidden life in Him in the obscurity of faith going out into the world as a river of living water.

We only see Him, All in all, and in seeing Him, we are ourselves in fullness.

And all this is accomplished by the Spirit of the Lord, and not by us. We don't touch it. We don't try to make it happen. This is something we cannot make happen in any way by any efforts of our own. It is a gift of God.

The growth I've found is not what I expected it to be a long time ago. I really thought I would become a more

28

loving person, more holy, more fervent, more caring, more more more more -- than I thought I was.

But since having found that "I" would never, ever, be able to produce the "self-improvements" I thought I needed, life has shifted inwardly from the stress of always striving to "become something one day" (but sadly never arriving), into a settled, continuous "I live yet not I but Christ lives" consciousness, which is subterranean to my moment-to-moment living and conscious thinking, and yet able to burst up into the present moment (forefront of my mind) at any time.

Now in that continuous "I live yet not I" life that is almost unconscious, I find myself just going around doing my daily business, whatever it is, and in doing my daily business, every moment is Christ, and that's the substance of my faith which is my real life that is within me.

We see indeed by revelation that all things consist of the Christ, the Word of God.[40] Scripture testifies to this over and over and we find it true in the depths of our being. And since there is no past or future in God, and since He is the God of the Living,[41] then He is the God of the Present. Therefore in the Present He exists in all His fullness, and in the Present By Him ALL THINGS consist, and in the Present Jesus sits at the right hand of the Father, and is also the Lamb in the midst of the Throne and the Bright and Morning Star. Also in the present moment, we sit in the midst of the throne with Him, to reign with Him, and by His gift to join with Him in being the vessel of the Father's life in the world we live in.

This is a continuous thing. This is the "already are-ness" we join when we come to who we are.

Yes, absolutely we are changed from day to day and from image to image. But what does Paul say? He says, "from glory to glory." He does not say from "worse" to "better," or from "lesser" to "more," or from "less perfect" to "more perfect." Paul says that we grow from one "glory" to another "glory" -- and that's all it is – it's all glory!

As we go from one consciousness to another, from one understanding to another, it is all Christ in His perfection every step of the journey, every moment! Every moment!

So the gist of it is not to see our growth as some sort of self-improvement, or getting better or holier, more loving, or even as becoming "closer" to God, but as Christ being as He means to be in us in the present moment.

If we believe He lives in us to will and to do of His good pleasure, then what other confession could we make?

We look into the mirror and what do we see? Paul says we see Christ when we look into a mirror. But when we look into a mirror we see ourselves. So then it is Christ in His own completion in ourselves in the here and now. We see what appears to be us in the mirror, but Paul says what we see is Christ. It is Christ reflecting Himself in us NOW.

As we always say, "*TODAY is the day of salvation. Today, if you will hear his voice...*"

Our job isn't to look at ourselves, to rate our progress, to consider our status, but simply to look "unto Him" continuously by faith as the Real Self Who is hidden in ourselves, and in the simplest of childlike faith we say, "Now I lay me down to sleep, I pray the Lord my soul to keep." And He does, "*For I know whom I have believed, and am persuaded that he is able to keep that which I have committed unto him against that day.*"[42]

Isn't that it, though? Which of us can know the way? There are a billion voices out there, all shouting something different, all purporting to be The Truth, and what certainty do we have over any other that the way we have found is THE way?"

O God, you're the ONLY ONE who knows! And You keep us in Your bosom, as the apple of Your eye, and promise to lead us and guide us and to receive us into glory!"

Shout hallelujah! We are back on the mercy train, the grace train, the only train in town!

And thank God our God is the Father of mercies. *"Blessed is the man unto whom the LORD imputeth not iniquity."*[43]

So of course, yes, we change, but how we change is like the Spirit, *"The wind bloweth where it listeth, and thou hearest the sound thereof, but canst not tell whence it cometh, and whither it goeth: so is every one that is born of the Spirit."*[44]

And also --

Mark 4:26
And he said, So is the kingdom of God, as if a man should cast seed into the ground;

27 And should sleep, and rise night and day, and the seed should spring and grow up, he knoweth not how.

28 For the earth bringeth forth fruit of herself; first the blade, then the ear, after that the full corn in the ear."

He knoweth not how" ... The seed grows up of itself, and becomes the full corn because it is its nature to do so. The Divine Seed has birthed Himself in you and in me and has brought Himself into the fullness of the Godhead bodily in us, and we "knoweth not how."

2, Pet. 1:4

O praise God. It is the Divine Nature in us, which grows up, of its own accord, in fullness.

We rejoice in today. Tomorrow will take care of the things of itself.

Christ's Mass (Or Incarnation)

Israel was not allowed to make images of God because God is not "out there" where we can look at Him.

Jesus came so that we would all come into the image of God in which we were created. God is the One Person Who is in and at the foundation of all of us. Each of us is a different and distinct living expression of the One Person. We all reflect the same One Image in each of us individually. This is the most astounding thing in the entire universe!

There is only one image of God -- the Christ of God reflected in you and me. There is no other image of God or other likeness. And the life of resurrection is the resurrected Life of Christ in our normal selves.

The heart cry of Moses: *Would God that all the LORD'S people were prophets, and that the LORD would put his spirit upon them!*[45] is fulfilled in Emmanuel, God with (in) us.

We are each the image of God that shines in our world. God enters the world by us. We are His opening to the world of Himself as He really is.

And God is Love. John says if we love our brother, we are in Him, for God is love.

"No man hath seen God at any time. If we love one another, God dwelleth in us, and his love is perfected in us."[46]

No man has ever seen God. John says this to our ears in plain English. Then "what" is God, if He can never be seen?

He is You and I loving each other. *cp. 1 Jn. 4:8*

We will never take it any farther than that, nor will it ever have a deeper meaning. (We might want to quibble on that and offer "definitions" of the person of God as an argument against something so intangible as "love," but no definition of the "Person of God" offered could have any credibility if the reality of love is not present, and if the love exists but we can't seem to find the proper definition behind it, I would trust the love more than the definition.)

There will never be a more "objective God" than the love you live in that flows from you out of your belly.

When it says it flows out of your belly, it means that it is a natural outflow of the life you live. The individual members of the Church grow up in their consciousness into the Head, which is Christ, and become organically One Eternal Person expressed by many different created persons. To be organically One Person means that we spontaneously bear the fruit of the Vine in the relaxation of simply being ourselves, having trusted the Invisible One to manifest Himself into visibility by the natural flow of the Sap (Holy Spirit) from the Vine into the Branches, which we are.

It means that you forget yourself. The scriptures say, *"When my father and my mother forsake me, then the LORD will take me up."*[47] This has more than a fleshly meaning. Our "father and mother" are our earthly dependence. We rely on them to support our earthly life, to insure our survival. But only until adulthood. When we are adults in this world, we are expected to go out into the world, leave dependence on our mother and father and to make our own lives.

To be an adult means that the focus of our lives becomes centered not on our own survival, but on giving life to and sustaining life for others. We become secondary to ourselves, and those for whom we are responsible become primary. We live to insure their lives. That is human life in maturity.

Spiritually, it means that whatever supports of self-will or repositories of self-reliance we had reserved for ourselves (earthly parents) are gone. They are done away with, and we learn that there is nothing in this world or the next, that can hold us up, except the Invisible Living God, Who is our True Self.

"Whosoever he be of you, that forsaketh not all that he hath, he cannot be my disciple."[48] The only "thing" we have is ourselves.

To forsake "all that we have," therefore, is to declare Him All.

It is to be "crucified," to see that we are "dead."

Our lives are hidden in Christ in God, and when we see Him, we shall be like Him, for we shall see Him as He is. Where do we look to see Him?

He is not "lo here or lo there." "It" (the kingdom of God, Christ) is "within you," which means that God has no geographical location, except as manifested in You.

You cannot look around and catch any glimpse of Him.

But everywhere you look He is all you see.

He is you. You are yourself.

The Same person???

Bingo!

According To Your Faith

"According to your faith be it unto you."[49] This can be a scary verse, depending on how you take it. But increasingly I realize this is an immutable law that is always operative. Therefore the world before and in us is always a product of our faith. This is an absolute fact. Where does this lead us?

I've always been moved by a story Agnes Sanford told in her autobiography, <u>Sealed Orders</u>. She grew up the child of missionaries in a missionary community in China. An event that greatly shaped her future occurred when one of the young missionary wives went into a dark depression from which she could not escape. As her depression worsened over time, the missionary community tried everything it could think of to bring her out of it. They prayed, they fasted, treated her medicinally as best they knew how, but in the end put it off on her. She wasn't healed, they told her, because she didn't have faith to be healed. Her depression was her fault, as well as her lack of deliverance. After that, Agnes relates, the young woman went into despair so black that she committed suicide. The good that occurred from it was that it drove Agnes, in subsequent years, to find the true Source for healing and compassion, and she went on to have a renowned healing ministry and to author many books.

We all know situations where a person has been beat over the head with his supposed lack of faith, because he did not exhibit physical healing, changed circumstances, or improved moral behavior.

Compassion compels us to want to find an answer other than to say to someone: "It's all your fault."

Yet we are faced square in the eyeballs with words from the scriptures that can't have any other than a literal meaning.

Like, *"according to your faith be it unto you,"* quoted above. Or, *"Therefore I say unto you, What things soever ye desire, when ye pray, believe that ye receive them, and ye shall have them."*[50]

Part of that verse also includes: *"and shall not doubt in his heart, but shall believe that those things which he saith shall come to pass; he shall have whatsoever he saith."*[51] Then there's Paul praying three times for a thorn to be removed from his side, and seemingly surprised that after THREE prayers for the same thing he hasn't had deliverance.

I'm thinking, Paul prayed only three times??? And for only one thorn??? How 'bout the thousands of times I've prayed for deliverance from my pincushion full of thorns? Is there something wrong with me, if Paul could be satisfied with his answer after only three prayers, while mine have gone on almost nonstop for years and years and years? *"My tears have been my meat day and night, while they continually say unto me, Where is thy God?"*[52]

Are you like me, (if we're having an honest moment), where these scriptures almost seem to mock us, mock what we "believe"? We do believe them, but do we fulfill them? I've never made a mountain pick up and cast itself into the sea, and don't know anyone who has to my knowledge.

One time back in the mid-seventies, when I was part of a Pentecostal church, we had a clogged sink in our rented house. So I called the landlord's handyman and he came out to fix it. Being the aggressive evangelist I was in those days, I found out that he was Jewish. So the thought occurred to me how great a miracle would be to demonstrate Jesus for this young Jewish handyman. So before he took the trap off, I told him I would pray for the sink, and that God would unclog it. I had every confidence He would, too. (Why I hadn't thought of that before calling the handyman, I don't know.) But what better confirmation of my witness to this young Jewish fellow than Jesus demonstrating Himself by the miraculous unclogging of a P-trap?

So, I leaned under the sink, laid hands on the P-trap, closed my eyes, and prayed. It was a great prayer, with all the right words and emotional fervency. The young Jewish handyman, obviously reared by his mama to be polite, kindly shielded the mirth in his eyes and was reverentially quiet during my prayer. When I finished, I told him to check the sink, and the drain would be unclogged.

Guess what!

Yep. Turned out it was still clogged. Uh-oh. Apparently the Lord wanted this one unclogged the old-fashioned way, but somehow I had not received that memo. And boy, did I look like a complete idiot. A religious fanatic crazy lunatic. Not to mention a very unsuccessful witness.

So, I've been a bit gun-shy since then. Wanted to make darn sure that if I declare a miracle, it was gonna happen.

But there is something inherently wrong in that thinking, isn't there? It's because "faith" has no guaranteed answer beforehand. It wouldn't be faith if it did. Faith, in any circumstance, is stepping out into the great wide open, where anything can happen, and nothing is certain.

What is faith? What does it do? How does it work?

In the mid 1800s a movement began in the United States, a push westward. It had been going on little by little since the nation's birth, but the discovery of gold and the prospect of free land caused a mammoth migration that eventually inundated the whole continent.

What was in the minds of the individual pioneers, as the first wispy tales of the mythical West reached their ears? The boundless skies, the rivers teeming with power and life, grasslands as far as the eye could see, mountains full of wildlife and endless beauty, bountiful meadows just waiting to be planted with the bread of life. It stirred their hearts, as the West's first European explorers, the "Mountain Men," told their tales to the settled folk back east.

And by the thousands they sold everything they had, bought Conestoga wagons and horse or oxen teams, joined wagon trains and began streaming into the vast uncharted wilderness that was the American West.

Many didn't make it and died on the way. Others made it to their destinations, but tragedy struck in other ways. But the vast majority did make it to their destinations or some stop along the way, and they built lives, towns and cities, and eventually the society we call this country.

How did they do it? Faith.

They heard the dream. It stirred their hearts. Families talked about it, prayed about it, until eventually they came to the crucial decision: "We're selling everything, and it's 'California or Bust.' We may meet enemies on the way, outlaws or hostile Indians. We may run out of food before we get there. Our horses may die or our wagons may break. But by hook or by crook, we're going!"

So they went. But not only did they have faith for the going, they had faith for what they would do when they got there. They had envisioned the farms and ranches they would carve out of Paradise, and the towns and cities that would follow. And true to their vision, the West conformed itself over the past one hundred fifty years to the vision of those pioneers, and far beyond what they saw.

This is a perfect example, in the natural, of faith and how it operates.

Faith starts with the seed of a dream. It may be wispy at first, and hard to define. But we feel its stir in our deepest places, where we can't quite put our finger. It comes from somewhere beyond, from some deeper place inside us than we ourselves are, and eventually comes to the forefront to confront us with its decisive moment. The moment of entering into faith is sometimes as cataclysmic and poignant as our wedding ceremony, because it portends to a complete change of life.

We've all no doubt heard how faith is like the act of sitting in a chair. Prior to our sitting down, there is no guarantee the chair will hold us. The decisive "moment" of faith is when we reach the point of no return in bending our knees and placing our posterior on the chair. Once having sat, the chair -- that object in which we had placed our "faith" (also known as our "buttocks") -- now holds us. What we had "trusted in uncertainty," has now, by our commitment to sitting, proved itself reliable by holding us up in our relaxation in it. We have now become our faith.

Now we come to the place of "sitting" in God. There is no one more "invisible" than God. No one more unproveable, more undetectable to the human mind or senses. But having now seen ourselves by faith through the Cross as having died and risen with Him, we have found Him to be reliably the True Self of our human selves, which express Him. Our first expressions and experiences of faith testify to the fact that God Himself now lives in us, and has overcome the wicked one.

And now in this new life, we are called to be "kings and priests" unto God. Having found our "All" in Him and forgetting ourselves (for "we" have been taken care of), living in Him Who is our Only Sufficiency, we are ready to speak the word of faith for the world we live in.

And this is the lesson for us from the history of the American West.

Your faith, which comes out of your dreams and visions in remembered moments, builds the world. We are not speaking of the faith that got you "saved" or caused you to "know your union." The faith we are speaking of here is the faith that goes out, unconcerned for itself, to build a city that it sees afar off. It may not see every step on the way, and it knows that dangers are part of the journey. It doesn't even know if it will survive until the end. But this faith has foundations, not in a temporal building of wood, brick and mortar, but in an eternal building, whose foundation is the unknowable Living God.

Your faith, in the slightest matter, changes the whole fabric of the universe. The universe is unlimited Freedom at its basis. Your faith operates the Freedom into coherency, into form, into the expressed Love of God.

But what IS faith? Heb 11:1

It is that decisive moment. THE Word. The "I will." BELIEVE!

God's "Will" is His "faith." What He "wills" becomes Reality.

It is the same with us. The pioneers said, "I will" when they sold their property and signed up for wagon trains. That "I will" propelled them into the wilderness, battling sicknesses, starvation and thirst, and attacks by enemies in

41

the night and day. That "I will" brought them to the lands they tamed and settled. Their "I will" shaped the society we now call America.

In the same way, and even more so and for even more eternal fruit, our faith "I will" changes the world. We do not seek a temporal society, or even temporal solutions. We are the pilgrims in Hebrews 11, who see a city afar off, whose builder and maker is God. We build an eternal city. A city unseen in the heavens. But which fills this whole earth even now.

Therefore everything we see in faith is not seen in the way of this world. But that does not make it less true. We have believed the Only True One, Who IS All in all. And we have been translated into an entirely new kingdom, right on the spot where we stand, where *nothing shall hurt nor destroy in all my holy mountain, for the earth shall be full of the knowledge of the LORD, as the waters cover the sea.*[53]

Now our privilege, as Kings and Priests unto God[54] who hold royal commissions in the Court of the Lord, is to declare the decrees that come out of Eternity. As our earthly forefathers sensed the dream of the freedom of the West, even so do we sense the stir of the dream of the ultimate Freedom of God, bursting at its seams in our inner selves, building pressure like an inner volcano in us, waiting for the right moment to erupt in flames and clouds to engulf the world we live in.

The Word of God, Christ in us, is now "our" Word. All the tensions and strains in our lives are building in each instance into the outgoing Word, the Word by which the world by us is blessed and reconciled to God.

That means that every word we have spoken and continue to speak will come to pass. Without fail. Today, tomorrow, next week, next year – it doesn't matter. Time is not the issue. Even if it seems to be. HE is the issue. "*Yea, let God be true and every man a liar.*"[55]

   According to your faith is it unto you.

Take, Eat, This Is My Body

And as they were eating, Jesus took bread, and blessed it, and brake it, and gave it to the disciples, and said, Take, eat; this is my body.[56]

John 6:

53 Then Jesus said unto them, Verily, verily, I say unto you, Except ye eat the flesh of the Son of man, and drink his blood, ye have no life in you.

54 Whoso eateth my flesh, and drinketh my blood, hath eternal life; and I will raise him up at the last day.

55 For my flesh is meat indeed, and my blood is drink indeed.

56 He that eateth my flesh, and drinketh my blood, dwelleth in me, and I in him.

57 As the living Father hath sent me, and I live by the Father: so he that eateth me, even he shall live by me.

Today I got up and went to work. I came home and went to the grocery store. After that we made us some supper -- baked breaded chicken and roasted potatoes and vegetables (the frozen kind). Then we watched TV until my wife fell asleep. Nobody called on the phone, and now I'm here in front of this very challenging (to the writer) computer screen.

Normal day. (Except for the "nobody called" part.) Anyone else can substitute his or her own normal day. Same difference.

So what does the dead and resurrected body and blood of a man who lived 2000 years ago have to do with the life I just described above? And how could we eat his flesh and drink his blood?

........I wrote the above passage a couple of weeks ago. I've spent the time since then mulling over these questions. I had to walk around in the question for a while.

There is what we might call an "academic" answer -- as lined out primarily by the apostle Paul in his epistles.

And that academic answer I know, and have taught others. But the question that struck me so profoundly is how can the "academic" facts, as laid out in Scripture, as revealed to us by the Spirit and through many Spirit-filled teachers, how do those "facts" touch me where I live every moment of my day? And to what purpose?

For "knowledge" of Christ cannot be simply memorized principles, no matter how true they are, because then they are no more than a philosophy by which we try to live our lives. "Knowledge" of Christ must be a Living Reality, permeating every molecule of our universe, for it is Christ Himself, and no mere "idea" of Him, that is our living truth.

In our union reality, we have come to see that through the Cross the Blood and Body of Jesus effects our salvation. We see that from the Garden, from our forefather Adam, we have been invaded in our inner center by self-centeredness, self-for-self, self-needing, which has its origins not in ourselves nor from some "fall" into a mere soulish existence, but in the father of lies who has built a hut in our inner selves. From that hut he broadcasts night and day, offering us this false mask of his making for our identity, seemingly standing up for our rights, but seeking only to ultimately produce wrath and enmity in us, for that is all he is, and he would have us be the same as he.

In the beginning Adam was Lord of this world. He had dominion over the earth. He spoke and the animals had names. He in some sense upheld the world. For as long as Adam and Eve had a pure vision of God, with no consciousness of anything but Him, they walked in Paradise, knowing no nakedness or shame. There was nothing to harm them, no enemy, and no sense of wrong of any kind. The earth was friend, and gave them her fruit in pleasant abundance.

When the trickster, Satan, gained a foothold in the Man, all the cosmos fell, too. The earth was "cursed" for his sake. Adam's vision of God, unconscious though it was, had sustained the world in paradise. Then his vision was ripped from him in the darkening of his understanding, and the heavens and the earth became the place he envisioned in his fear. And all the generations since have labored on that building of fear whose foundations were laid that day.

The way to make this personal is to realize that we are all Adam. Our life does not hinge on belief, one way or another, about that long ago Adam. It hinges on realizing we ourselves are Adam. I am Adam. His story is my story. Our story *Always?*

And likewise, everyone's story is my story and visa versa. One of the most insidious effects of this cracked consciousness is to not see that we each are the Same Person in all, that we are in some very real sense each other and joined together, and that what affects one affects all. Instead we see a chaotic disjointed mess of "individuals," all asserting and fighting for their own rights and needs.

Paul said that if we offend in one point of the law, we are guilty of all. That's a pretty inclusive statement. It puts everybody on an even keel. No hierarchies of "goodness." If offending in one point makes you guilty of all, then that makes somebody who lies to his mom about how much change he brought home from the store (which I did, and by far not the worst thing, either), equal to Adolph Hitler, in terms of being a lawbreaker. I'm the same as Hitler. So is everybody else.

What makes it the same for everybody is that the real lawbreaker is the Evil One. We all do our bout with him, all fall under his sway for a time, walking off with him with his friendly arm on our shoulder, believing his boasts and his bravado, only to find ourselves betrayed and where we never thought we would be, doing what we never thought we would do.

John the Baptist prophesied: *And now also the ax is laid unto the root of the trees: therefore every tree which bringeth not forth good fruit is hewn down, and cast into the fire. I indeed baptize you with water unto repentance: but he that cometh after me is mightier than I, whose shoes I am not worthy to bear: he shall baptize you with the Holy Ghost, and with fire.*[57]

John said the *"ax is laid unto the root of the trees."* He is saying that the Lord Jesus Christ, who was then still to come, would cast out the prince of this world, out from the hearts of men. He would take back that which was His own, to fill them with His own Spirit, and the all-consuming fire of His passion. This is God establishing man as His dwelling place, His Temple.

But in order to do that the usurper had to be cast out. Stolen territory had to be retaken. A land had to be remade. Minds had to be renewed.

Heb 10:

4 For it is not possible that the blood of bulls and of goats should take away sins.

47

5 *Wherefore when he cometh into the world, he saith,* *Sacrifice and offering thou wouldest not, but a body hast thou prepared me:*

6 *In burnt offerings and sacrifices for sin thou hast had no pleasure.*

7 *Then said I, Lo, I come (in the volume of the book it is written of me,) to do thy will, O God.*

"A body hast thou prepared me." Jesus Christ was, according to Paul, the fullness of the Godhead walking around bodily on the earth. That cannot make sense to fleshly ears. Fleshly ears and eyes think that God, like anybody else we can think of, has to be somewhere specific. So if He's in heaven, He isn't here, and if He's here, He can't be in heaven. But this isn't a case of either/or. It's both/and. Jesus was the complete fullness of the Godhead, walking around in a regular human body.

And thus it was a fully God-directed, God-empowered, human body. Jesus had known from His baptism what road He was to walk, what would happen, and what it was for. He, like Abraham before Him, could for a time only see a kingdom afar off, and always ahead an altar of sacrifice for the Lamb of God.

Jesus was God experiencing life and living completely as a human being in the world of fallen Adam. From the standpoint of origins, Adam was shaped in loving gentleness out of the elements of the earth, with Life breathed into his nostrils by the Lord God Himself. He was born into Innocence and Paradise.

Jesus, on the other hand, was born out of a woman in the travail and pain of bloody childbirth, in a stable, in a land far from Paradise. Shortly after his birth He was whisked away by his father into far-off Egypt to escape the slaughter of Herod. Adam was born in the surroundings of the most gentle, comforting nursery imaginable, while Jesus was born into a land of fear with good reason for the fear.

During His whole life Jesus surely absorbed all he heard, experienced and felt, everything which was common to humanity. But certainly after His commission by the Spirit, He felt in Himself, in His mind and body, all that the roiling masses, the "sheep without a shepherd," experienced in the depths of their minds and hearts. He was a "man of sorrows, acquainted with grief." Not just the grief of losing a loved one, or the sorrow of losing a lover, but the deep abiding sorrow that hides behind everything in this world.

Jesus' task was to take all that into Himself and to shine it all through and through with the glory of God. That was God's plan. In order to do that, He needed somebody to walk around on the earth and live in it, become one with it, die its death, and then raise it up into Himself as He really IS. So Jesus came walking around on the earth in a body born of this earth in order to do just that.

When Jesus was nailed to the Cross on Golgotha and raised for all to see, Paul says He *"was made sin for us, that we might be made the righteousness of God."*[58] In other words, in the Cross His complete "oneness" with the human race was accomplished, in that He became completely what humanity had become -- sin.

This is another of those actions of God that we tend to see in separated, purely judicial terms. In that thinking, Jesus dies, and God way off in heaven from His throne says, "Ok, I'll accept His death in place of everybody else's." But again, this is more than a judicial decree from a heavenly Throne. Jesus' death and subsequent resurrection are the actual means of the reconciliation of all things. Not by an arbitrary declaration, but by virtue of what was actually accomplished.

When Jesus took "sin" into Himself, "became sin," it can't mean any other thing but that the spirit of the power of the air, the spirit of wrath, the father of lies, the prince of this world, came crashing down into him with all the hatred and fury of unrestrained Hell. Jesus had taken upon Himself, by the Spirit, the role of sin-bearer, the scapegoat who bears the sins of the people outside the camp into the wilderness.[59] He knew in Himself that He was one Person with all of humanity. He was the Root and Offspring of David,[60] meaning He was both God and Man, Source and Manifestation.

Therefore, being the Same One Person with us all, the Light that lights every man that comes into the world, only He could by His own will take all the ravages of Hell into Himself. All of humanity is in Him, not just figuratively, but as literally as can be. Only He could let Hell have its full fury, vent the fire of its rage, against the Man that God had made in His image. Only He was safe enough, in all the universe, to take the fullness of sin into Himself, to be made sin, and subsequently to go in the thrall of death into the deepest depths of sin and hell, hatred, wrath, enmity, strife, pride, envy, covetousness, weeping and gnashing of teeth, wails of pain, cries of insane devilry and mimicking laughter with no end.

When He was made what we had become, had borne all we would bear, and had descended into the deepest depths of darkness in *the lower parts of the earth*," Paul says *"He that descended is the same also that ascended up far above all heavens, that he might fill all things."*[61] All things. Even death and hell.

Jesus took all mankind with Him into that death. We were there, not just figuratively, but actually, in the Spirit, which is the true reality. And in that death, *"he led captivity captive,"* and was afterward raised by the power of the Father.

When He rose from the tomb the third day, He had won. The enemy of our souls had been vanquished; his kingdom was condemned to death. He was shown to be the impotent liar he really is. Because his greatest triumph, dividing asunder God and man, had been made null and void -- the veil of the temple was split in two.

The veil of the temple is the symbol of what separated mankind from God. God was behind the veil, and no flesh could approach. Mankind was sinful, unclean, unholy, and could not look upon nor approach the Holy God. It was the veil the enemy put on Adam and Eve in the Garden that caused them to be afraid of God and ashamed of their nakedness. It was the same veil that was on the children of Israel at Mt. Sinai, when Moses went up to receive the law, and they could not even so much as touch the mountain, because they were afraid they would die. It was the same veil that was over the eyes of the ten scouts who were sent to spy out the land of Canaan, who came back having seen giants in the land and themselves only as grasshoppers in their own sight.[62]

It is the veil of separation, of self which is only separated in its devil-induced consciousness, but with power enough in that delusion to create a whole separate, but false reality.

And it is the same veil we are all born with, that is over our eyes until the day comes we see the death and resurrection of Jesus in ourselves. With a sound like a clap of thunder right over our house, the roof is blown off our minds, the walls surrounding our hearts come down, and like a rushing mighty wind that is at the same time a gentle cool breeze in the springtime, we come to "know" God in the inner intimacy of His Spirit joined with ours, so that we find we are Christ living in our flesh.

Jesus took sin into His body unto death, and rose again in His body unto life, and brought our whole race and the heavens and the earth into that life of reconciliation and oneness with God. Though all is not yet seen that He accomplished.[63]

When Jesus arose, and brought all mankind with Him, He arose to a new kingdom. What had been lost in Adam, Jesus restored. He restored the kingdom of God in man. He cleansed the temple of man that he might be a fit dwelling place for the Glory of God's presence. He sent sin out into the wilderness -- indeed as far as the east is from the west.

When the Son said, "*Lo, I come to do thy will O God*" and "*a body hast thou prepared me,*"[64] the author says that the new covenant means this: "*By the which will [covenant] we are sanctified through the offering of the body of Jesus Christ once for all.*"[65] And "*For by one offering he hath perfected for ever them that are sanctified.*"[66]

In the body of Christ, by the filling of that body with the power and person of the Spirit, we are raised with Him completely into a new kingdom, a new creation, which isn't really new, because it is just things as they really are. But it is new because we are now, and everyday, seeing it for the first time. This is not a mental game, a philosophical feel-good mantra that we repeat over and over, but the Truth. In Him, in His Kingdom into which we have been translated by the death and resurrection of the Son, there is nothing to hurt nor harm. We ARE His Holy Mountain. Sin and the author of sin, the devil, do not exist in His Holy Mountain. They have no power there. And we live there always.

The veil of the temple has been rent in twain. The division (sin, devil, separation) between God and man has been removed. Gone. God considers it not. In the blood of Christ Jesus all consciousness of sins is removed, and in His death and resurrection we die with him forever to sin and rise with Him forever to righteousness.

I asked the question in the beginning of this how could these long ago events truly affect me in my daily regular human living, and how could I drink His blood and eat His flesh?

The answer to both questions is the same. When the temple veil was split in two, and the barrier between man and God was removed, we were taken in Him into the Holy of Holies, into the Throne, where Paul says we sit with Him in heavenly places. But only priests can go into the temple holy places, and only the High Priest into the Most Holy. Therefore, since our Redeemer is also forever our High Priest, who *"ever liveth to make intercession for us,"*[67] and we have been brought into His most intimate presence, it can only mean that we, too, have been called into the same calling. The Presence of God is not just for bliss and joy and meditation. God is an outgoing Will to Love, to Give Life, to Bless, to Redeem and Reconcile.

To live by feeding off Him, to drink His blood and to eat His flesh, is the stuff of everyday life. Jesus said, *"My meat is to do the will of Him who sent me, and to finish His work."*[68]

If we are found in Him, then we are no longer shut-ins looking out only for our own welfare. Our spiritual well being, as well as our physical, emotional, intellectual "needs" are now met in Him Who is All in all. It isn't about us anymore. It isn't about getting ourselves straight. It isn't about getting our needs met.

Paul said we eat and drink the Lord in remembrance of His death til He comes. What -- just as some sort of memorial service? No -- God forbid! To eat and drink in remembrance of His death is to realize that all that comes my way, to challenge me, to try me, to pull me here and pull me there, is the continuance of the dying of the Lord Jesus in my body, that He might be manifest in my mortal flesh.

Though Jesus' death and resurrection completed all things, we are called and privileged to be sharing in the *"filling up that which is behind of the sufferings of Christ,"*[69] which is saying that our lives are individually a part of the fulfillment of His faith and what He accomplished. We are part of the manifestation and fulfillment of His "filling all things."

The blood of Christ we drink in the new kingdom we now walk in, is the blood of the forgiveness of sins, not primarily our own, but now those of others. His blood courses through every fiber of our new being. All things are purged in His blood, and our consciences are cleansed and purified continuously in Him.[70] With this clear vision of love pouring out of our inner center, we testify to the blood of Christ by pronouncing peace where God sends us. We are His forgiveness manifest in the world.

When we eat His flesh we ascend with Him in the Resurrection, to oneness with God, oneness with Christ, oneness with the Spirit, for we consume Him as the Living Bread which came down from Heaven, so that all that He is becomes part and parcel of all that we are, and from that continuous eating the Divine Essence flows through every molecule of our spirits, souls and bodies, hiddenly quickening life in our mortal bodies and inwardly renewing our inner selves day by day by day by day.

And God sheds abroad His love in our hearts not for naught, for Love IS purpose, and we eat Him as the Lamb slain so that we, too, are the Lamb slain, in this world, in our time, right here, right now, in whatever state or moment we are caught reading these words.

One of the greatest temptations I've had with hearing this is that it sounds so Pollyannaish, so head-in-the-sand-ish, to believe that all that happens to me is for others, when it sure seems like there are lots of pickles "I" got myself into. "Well this is another fine kettle of fish." It's lots easier to believe stuff is "my fault," or that guy over there, his fault, but not that this human life that just seems kind of "normal" most of the time is really the laid-down life of the Christ of God. That me waiting too long in a red light is helping somebody somewhere, and not just testing my patience. That's far-out; you have to admit.

And this is where we take the same "leap of faith" that I believe Jesus also took. To believe that we are one with God, who is the same Person in all, also means that we are one with each other. Jesus had to reach out in faith to grasp the being of man, to embrace all mankind within

Himself, to say that our hurts were His hurts, our diseases His diseases. He took all of that with Him to the Cross. And it was another leap of faith to throw Himself fully into God in letting the full force of Hell violate Him. It was a leap of faith to be in the darkest separation beyond the bounds of our imagination, when He could not see the face of the Father looking at Him, and to say out of the pit of the hell that had started to overtake Him, "*My God, my God, why hast thou forsaken me?*" It was a leap of faith for Him to say, "*It is finished*" and to "*give up the ghost.*" To go all the way into death.

And it was a leap of faith made beforehand, that trusted the Father's Promise, that He only knew by the Scripture and the quickening of the Spirit, that "*thou wilt not leave my soul in hell; neither wilt thou suffer thine Holy One to see corruption.*"[71]

To eat His flesh is to enter into the law of the harvest: "*Except a corn of wheat fall into the ground and die, it abideth alone: but if it die, it bringeth forth much fruit.*"[72]

God has not called us to comfort, ease, or emotional bliss in a mystical state. He has called us to be Who He is, and He is the Will and Power of Love, which means He takes any shape, uses any means, dies any death, endures any hardship, suffers loss, wrong, pain and injustice, and wears any disguise, in His One Eternal Project, to reproduce Himself by and through love throughout the whole of creation.

Those who have drunk His blood and eaten His flesh are the very Sacrifice of God poured out for the world. They are the mercy of God that extends from sea to sea, covering all.

A Second Little Word on Faith

Genesis 25:

"7 And these are the days of the years of Abraham's life which he lived, an hundred threescore and fifteen years.

8 Then Abraham gave up the ghost, and died in a good old age, an old man, and full of years"

Perhaps it might seem I have relegated faith to special times and especially difficult situations.

And rightly so, for it is that. There are indeed special moments, when God speaks as a thunderclap in our being. These are the moments that under gird the rest of our lives.

But what about the rest of the time? The times when we are just living, doing the things we do -- working our jobs, picking up the kids, taking the car in for repair, mowing the lawn, and the thousand other "mundane" things we do every day? Days when there is no "special word" from God that day; it's just the day that followed the day before and lived pretty much like every other day we can remember.

That's why I noticed Abraham's life. Isaac, we all know, was born when Abraham was one hundred years old, Sarah ninety. The Promise that God gave Abraham had occurred twenty-five years earlier, and after the Promise was fulfilled in the birth of Isaac, Abraham lived another seventy-five years. For my money, that's a lot of time. What in the world was he doing all that time?

Just being a desert patriarch I suppose. Whatever it was that a desert patriarch did all day. Maybe check out the sheep herd, the supply of dates and wine, fix tents, camel saddle repair, etc.

But my point is this. Life is mostly not those rough moments. Those times come, and strength in those moments is found in Christ in a way beyond what we know. But it isn't those moments I'm talking about here.

It's the regular every-day real-life moments that seem like "just us" living when we're walking through the day in the consecutive moments of life, just being "ourselves" with maybe no particular thoughts of God. Dealing with traffic. Fighting for our rights at fast-food restaurants ("I said NO onions"). Opening the mail. Watching the weather. Arguing over the phone with adult children. Cooking supper. Taking out the trash. Catching the game.

Here is the crux of the matter, where the rubber meets the road. Because, wonderful as they are, experiences on the Mount of Transfiguration are rare. Really low lows followed by really high highs are not the norm. Life is mostly just "in-between." And the "in-between" is the sanctified life.

From the moment of God's pronouncement upon Abram that his faith was counted as righteousness, the sanctity of God fell upon the whole of Abram's existence. All of Abram's life was the life of God's Spirit in action. His name became Abraham -- "father of many nations." But he was just living as a regular human person of his day.

Probably ninety percent or more of Abraham's life was spent just doing regular stuff, just like we ourselves do every day. It was different stuff, to be sure, than what we do. But it was just regular human living for his day, and life is the same in our day as well. And Abraham's "regular human living" was the life of God, Christ, being expressed in his patriarchal world.

The lesson for us is that once the stamp of God has been placed on our lives, from the moment we realize it and are carried along in the faith of God, God's sanctity rules our lives. It doesn't matter whether we're grilling burgers in the backyard or preaching to heathens on remote islands, the same Christ is operating fully as ourselves in our daily lives, in each moment of our daily lives, and all for <u>His own</u> redemptive purposes.

And by redemptive I mean a continual calling forth of life in the midst of what appears to be deaths of different sorts all around us. I mean no "special thing" when I say a "continual calling forth of life." It is Who we are in the mundane as well as Who we are in the theophanied moments that is the same WHO in each, whether mundane or transfigured with visions. The very presence of ourselves IS the "continual calling forth of life" in redemption. Christ is All in all. I and my Father are one.[73]

So bottom line what I'm saying is this: Christ is Christ in the Monopoly Board and checkout line as much as He is Christ in the Deepest Heavens of the Father (for they are the same). In the resurrection life, which He is NOW living by us, He has sanctified all our existence. His sanctification of our lives is based on He living in us, and not on anything we could add to the equation.

God dwells in heaven. God dwells in us. Seeing heaven within us is seeing heaven everywhere. And seeing heaven everywhere is seeing God everywhere.

And this is a vision, not of sight, but of faith. Everyday faith. Unconscious faith, just living.

Today, believe the Truth -- Christ the Lord is being YOU today! This moment. *"I will dwell in them and walk in them and be their God."*

Faith on the Brink

Faith is the only means of "contact" with God.

We are often caught in thinking that something else is a means to God -- our behavior, our thoughts, our intents -- our our our our.

Faith is the only transcendence of all that.

Because faith brings us to a brink of complete darkness where there is only a black abyss ahead and the only recourse is to leap into it without any reasonable expectation of not falling to our death in the deep chasm below.

Why? Because "God" is a "no-thing." There is, so to speak, "nothing" to leap to. Our earthly parents caught us when we jumped off a chair when we were little. But there's nobody there now. We are alone. Nobody is around. There are no warm fuzzies. There is only a raw nakedness of "belief" in a "no-thing", which is neither felt nor perceived by the senses.

It is a complete leap into the unknown. This is why faith alone is the only "means" of contact with God, because of that complete stripping away of anything human -- "no flesh shall come into my Presence"[74] ... "by the works of the law shall no man be justified."[75]

Though Moses had seen with his fleshly eyes the miracles of God in plagues and deliverances, still every time the children of Israel brought difficult issues to him, he "fell on his face before the Lord". He became as if dead. Moses, like us, found increasingly that there was nothing in him, in his "flesh," that could come up with the answer, solve the problem, or prevail against a host of enemies. GOD ONLY was the solution.

To "fall on our faces before the Lord" is to leap into the invisible God without recourse to anything else. And then, every time, as with Moses and Ezekiel, we are caused to stand up.

Ezekiel 2:
"*1 And he said unto me, Son of man, stand upon thy feet, and I will speak unto thee.*
2 And the spirit entered into me when he spake unto me, and set me upon my feet, that I heard him that spake unto me."

When we are caused to stand up, then comes the commission and the empowerment.

"*3 And he said unto me, Son of man, I send thee to the children of Israel....* "

"I send thee". This is a different "I" from the one we heard in the to's and fro's of the doubts and fears that brought us to the death. That was a self-concerned "I," an "I" fearful for itself. But now this newly risen "I" speaks and says "I send thee!" The Divine Word explodes into the darkness and death in us; it floods everything around with Light and Power. We rise to our feet hearing the Word of God, which comes as wisdom, power, love, purpose, meaning, hope and direction.

"*This is the way, walk ye in it.*" Now the Word that took us to death, darkness and terror, becomes the Word that is "*a lamp unto my feet, and a light unto my path.*"[76]

And we thus know the next way to go, and that we will prevail. He wears a mask in the world that looks like you and me, and in those unlikely disguises He dispenses His grace, power and love wherever He walks as us.

Isn't this true?

Abraham and Isaac in the Land of Moriah

Isaac was the fulfillment of Abraham's long-awaited desire for an heir. Ninety-nine years of Abraham's life led up to the birth of Isaac. After all that, you'd think it would be smooth sailing from then on out. No way.

In Genesis 22, God tells Abraham to take Isaac to a mountain in the land of Moriah, and there to offer him up for a burnt offering. So Abraham rounds up Isaac, two young men servants, some donkeys, wood, fire, provisions and a knife to kill the sacrifice, and they set out for the land of Moriah, where God will tell him which mountain to use for the sacrifice.

"Then on the third day Abraham lifted up his eyes, and saw the place afar off."[77]

The third day, eh? There is no record of their conversation the previous two days. But on the third day, the first thing Abraham says is to the servants:

"Abide ye here with the ass; and I and the lad will go yonder and worship, and come again to you."[78]

For three days Abraham has been walking, holding the knife in his hand that he will plunge into his son Isaac. Abraham died to anything else the moment he heard God's word. He just gathered his party and provisions and set out on the road. Three days he must've walked, three days maybe of inward weeping, of hopelessness yet determination, of questioning why this had to be, yet walking step by step toward the mountains in the distance.

They must have been black nights under the clear stars of Canaan. Their tents must have been quiet. Neither the servants nor Isaac knew the true nature of their journey, but Abraham couldn't completely conceal the grimness that had seized his bones, which surely put a morbid pall on their encampment. Yet in the midst of Abraham's hell were whispers of hope, barely heard, barely clung to.

But the third day he lifted up his eyes and saw the place afar off.

What did he see? He saw the mountain of sacrifice. Where the lamb of God would be slain. Where the Son of God would rise from the dead.

The third day was the resurrection. Abraham died when the word of the Lord came to him to kill Isaac, and rose again on the third day when he lifted up his eyes and saw the place afar off.

Only then could he speak his prophetic word that, *"I AND the lad will go -- and come again unto you."*

He didn't know how, he didn't have a clue. He planned to go through with the plan, to tie Isaac up, bind him to an altar, and plunge a knife into him. The plan was sealed. But even so, Abraham saw beyond that to the resurrection of Christ.

I'm not talking about Jesus' resurrection in Palestine two thousand years ago, though of course it means and points to that. I'm talking about the resurrection taking place in the midst of death right now. My death. Your death. Anybody's death.

Abraham in his own death died to Isaac as well, to anything but God Himself. Isaac died for him the moment

God told him to do it and he agreed to it. That was a foregone conclusion.

But the third day he saw the place afar off. Out of the mist the Living God arose, and the word welled up in Abraham in answer to Isaac's wondering about the sacrificial lamb, *"My son, God will provide Himself a Lamb for a burnt offering."*[79]

And still he marches up that mountain, having seen the vision of God, having received the word in his heart that he and Isaac will descend back down the mountain together. Still he ties Isaac with cords and binds him as a sacrifice to the altar. Still he raises the knife, with full intent to drive it into the chest of his only begotten son of promise. Even while "seeing the place afar off," he starts his downward thrust into the heart of love.

The angel stays his hand at that final moment, Isaac is freed, and a ram suddenly bleats from the bushes.

Jesus endured the cross, for the joy that was set before him.

When Abraham and Isaac were both "raised," God told Abraham again and Isaac that through his seed *"all nations would be blessed."*[80]

If a corn of wheat falls into the ground and dies, it brings forth much fruit. We are about resurrection. We are sent out to attain resurrection. Not only the resurrection of our bodies in the final day, but the resurrection of our brothers and sisters into the liberty of the sons of God in the here and now. Our final resurrection we see afar off. But today we are as sheep counted for the slaughter.

Maybe that sounds morbid but it isn't. It is the process of God's nature. To be in God's kingdom is to be in the flow of His resurrection, which springs out of death. Out of a cross.

But it is not the hopeless death of suicidal despair. His Word is your life in all, even in giving up the ghost and crying, *"My God, my God, why hast thou forsaken me?"* The word is alive in the secret place in the midst of your heart, *"I shall not die, but live, and declare the works of God,"*[81] and, *"For thou wilt not leave my soul in hell; neither wilt thou suffer thine Holy One to see corruption."*[82]

Yes, we are killed all the day long, counted as sheep for the slaughter. Not to perdition, but to resurrection!

We die to live, to give life. We bear about in the body daily the dying of the Lord Jesus, that the life of Jesus would be manifest in our mortal flesh.

Believe that and quit judging yourself. Have the faith of God. Everything in your life is redemptive. Whatever it is. If you think you got yourself into the mess you're in, think again. He works all things after the counsel of His own will.[83] The first of the four spiritual laws is true: God loves you and has a wonderful plan for your life. It is true!

You're in it right now. In the plan. And the plan for now is for you and I to continue to fill up that which is behind of the afflictions of Christ. Don't judge whether the stuff in your life is "worthy" to be called that. Leave it to God.

If you and He are one, if you live, yet not you but He lives your life, then your whole life is nothing but His self-giving love, because that is what He is. And He is still enduring the cross, despising the shame, in and as you and me for the redemption of the world. In whatever we do.

And resurrection will come! Why? Because in the midst of that cross the inner Word came to you, and you lifted up your eyes and saw the place afar off.

Believe the Word He has spoken to you.

God Will Provide

My son, God will provide himself a lamb for a burnt offering.[84]

What has so powerfully overwhelmed me is the word "HIMSELF."

Let's not forget the Lamb IS God. God to the rescue out of the utter weakness, vulnerability and willingness-to-be-killed of a little helpless lamb.

And let's not forget that we are not separate from our Father, Who sends us as lambs to the slaughter.

Yet not we, but He. When He sends us, He Himself goes.

But being sent like a lamb to the slaughter feels like separation. It feels like we are outside of God, or have been abandoned by Him.

We walk on anyway. The word of faith we have heard and spoken inwardly energizes us and propels us onward to an unseen impossible goal. To live.

At the last minute no separate lamb appears. GOD HIMSELF is the Lamb who comes out of nowhere and takes the death unto Himself. In apparent separation (in our minds) we think we are going down to die, and hope is like a wispy dream, but at the last minute another comes to take the death in us.

God will provide HIMSELF -- as a lamb.

And the risen Son who is ourselves (Christ in us) will be the seed that blesses all nations. (And by "all nations," I don't mean something grandiose. I just mean all the life around us as far as we extend ourselves into it.)

God has only provided one "thing" in the universe: Himself. He is the Source out of which everything not only appears, but also is held up as a Living Reality moment by moment.

Whom have I in heaven but thee? And there is none upon earth I desire beside thee. My heart and my flesh faileth, but God is the strength of my heart, and my portion forever.[85]

One Garden

We have previously spoken to the fact that the foundation of the entire universe is simply this: the whole is One Person, God, manifesting Himself through a variety of innumerable forms which He created out of His Word.[86] Indeed, God is the Life in all that is. And that One Person, again says the apostle John, is "Love," which means the fulfillment of His Life is found in giving life to others.

Consider a flower garden, lush and verdant in the fullness of summer. Over here you have pansies, hydrangeas, marigolds, while over there are bountiful impatiens, zinnias, and amaranth. Besides the sheer beauty of it, the garden is a literal beehive of activity, as all sorts of creatures take sustenance and shelter in it.

But where does it come from, this overwhelming lushness of color and life? Each flower grows from a different seed; each seed derives its life from the soil and the water in the soil, but it is Sunlight that makes the garden grow and come to fruition. Each seed grows according to its own inner code, "after its own kind," the Bible says, but it is the same Sun in each. The Sunlight is the inner life of the whole garden, giving life to every individual part of it. Leave the seed, soil, and water, and take away the Sun, and you have no garden. So, we might say, our garden is "Sunlight manifesting itself in a multitude of individual forms." What does the sunlight exist for? Not for itself, just to manifest sunlight, but instead to manifest itself as the plants and animals and other life that only exists because of its outpouring.

And this is the sense in which we mean that the entire universe is One Person manifesting Himself. He is the Ground of Being for all that is. As Paul said to the Greeks in Athens, *"For in Him we live and move and have our being."*[87]

Shadows and Light

I always like it when God shows me a picture. Like the saying says, it's worth a thousand words. Today's picture was no exception.

I work in St. Matthews, Kentucky, one of the first and most well kept suburbs in Louisville. Parts of it are absolutely gorgeous. Huge aged hardwood trees billow over most of the residential streets.

This day was a day of extra intense sunshine, and as I was driving through the tree-lined streets, on my right I approached a yard into which somehow the sunshine had collected in force, in vivid contrast to all the shadowed lawns around it. Everything in the clear space between the trees glowed as if all the light was originating from that spot. The yard was almost as if transfigured.

Right before that scene I had been thinking about how everyone is a child of God, though not necessarily (yet) a son. All are His offspring, as Paul said to the Athenians. I was thinking how like calls to like, in that Christ – "the light that lights every man that comes into the world" -- lies dormant like a seed in every man, until that seed is called forth somehow by Christ to spring into life. So whether dormant and yet to live, or living now as sons, I saw all humanity in the light of God's seed coming to birth in each one. (I was not dealing with questions of doctrines or dogmas, about who will or who won't be saved, but rather with my own inner seeing of reality, and what the potentials are for everyone in the mind of the Father, and what I as a Son have permission to speak from God's mind.)

So while I was thinking on this, suddenly an unusually bright patch of light among deep shadows appeared. And there in that picture was my confirmation right on the spot.

Because what I saw was that the same reality that existed in the light also existed in the shadows. The only difference in the spot that was radiant was that the Light was shining there. So I saw that whether in the light, or in the shadow, it is the same substance. The light brings it out, brings it to life, gives it existence in consciousness, but the same potential for reality exists in the shadow and only needs the light to shine on it to make it manifest.

Well, that's our job, isn't it? The Sons are the Light of the world, and as such shine in the shadows to show forth the truth in every man, which lies dormant as a seed in Him until One speaks who calls him forth to the truth of who he is.

✕ Duality

"You have to experience duality for a long time until you see it's not there." Thomas Merton.

How can you experience something that is not there?

I think the hold duality or "separation" has on us is because it is what seems real, and the "other" is suspect. It's all we've ever known. Therefore the ever-present task before us is to jump over that duality/separation in our faith. But truthfully, we really don't know how to do even that.

I think those who say the material world is illusion miss the point. What we see is real, neither a trick nor an illusion. What we fail to see, however, is the unity and oneness that underlies everything.

But that is also its difficulty, because we do not deny what is before our eyes, what touches our senses, goes through our minds, or passes through our bodies. Life on earth is gut-wrenchingly REAL. (FACT)

Because this life is real, not illusion or dream, but real life being lived by real people in a real existence, the difficulty comes in seeing the wholeness which has interweaved all the contrary and opposing parts together. Each individual segment of this reality seems disjointed from the whole, and therefore the disjointedness, which is readily apparent, seems to be its main feature, (disjointedness being separation).

The fact that reality is an unbroken wholeness of flesh/matter and spirit/heaven is not apparent. We always want to separate flesh and spirit. We know flesh "by itself" doesn't work. Neither (as it relates to us) does "spirit" work

74

"by itself." "*When you see Me you see the Father*" -- flesh
AND spirit = ONE.

It isn't that we don't see the reality before us, but that
we do not see the fact that it is whole, perfect and safe
— and not fragmented, chaotic and unfriendly. When you
live "in the Spirit" as it says in Romans 8, flesh and spirit
are one, the one (flesh) manifesting the other (Spirit). To
live "in the flesh," is to live as if flesh and spirit are two, each
being the other's enemy and living in perpetual conflict.

cp. Rom. 8:8 *yes*

This "living in the Spirit" means that we can live in
liberty and wholeness, flesh and spirit not contrary one
to the other. The Lord has taken the "fragmented parts"
(which were only fragmented in our sight, anyway, since
nothing was ever really fragmented) and shown us that
HE is the All in all in every thread and fiber, every color
and every design of the eternal tapestry that is each of
our lives. And that means that our flesh is now Christ
manifesting Himself.

? see Galatians 5:16-17

Therefore our "flesh," (our human-ness, humanity),
instead of being our lifelong enemy, has become the mortal
arena where Christ lives in His glory, and which He now
uses as His instrument to express His own quality of self-
for-others life.

inaccurate alternative

*→ P.33 * see "Jesus & Jargons" P.26,27*

No Containment Policy

There is a Zen saying I've always remembered from my former days: "If you meet the Buddha on the road, kill him!" What does that mean? It means there is no Buddha on the road – therefore it could only be a projection of your false ego's perception -- and by slaying the false Buddha you realize the only Buddha is you. In Christian terms, it means Christ is not "lo here, or lo there," i.e. some visible sign or person you can see and touch, but "within YOU."

What we have to offer is not a theological system that we can give someone, in five sessions, point by point, so that he or she can go home and apply the system and in fifteen weeks cause guaranteed life-changing results or your money back. Christ cannot be bottled and sold on the Internet, or in a weekend seminar.

The only "thing" we "offer" is Christ Himself as the only sufficiency for all things, including the foundation of and manifestation of <u>our very selves</u>. The "you" that is "you" is He!

It is, as my friend Bette Ketcham says, "He climbed up into me and became one Me with Him." This is the most distinct and certain shift in consciousness there can be, because it is His own mind, heart and self pouring out of the Godhead in love and grace filling this earthly vessel -- body, soul and spirit -- with Himself, thereby becoming "one" with us in completeness.

Everybody has to cross the threshold alone. We are caught up of the Spirit of Jesus who for a time leads us into the desert, until the day we realize, *"Arise, shine, thy light is come,"* and that *"I live, yet not I, but He lives, and now* <u>*I live as He living."*</u> Gal 2:20

76

Though a thousand witnesses would share that with us, still it isn't ours until the Spirit rises up in us at His appointed time and says it in us, and we know that He does.

How do we communicate this?

I would think if we would emulate anything of those who have gone before us, it would be to let the Spirit be free in each person in love. We give our part, which is our portion of the Living Christ, as we are given it. There is no defining in any way whatsoever how that will be. Let others give their part whatever it is. God will mesh it all together for the good of all.

How is it we can ever shift from "head knowledge" to just living? Think of driving a car? When we were first learning we were attentive to and nervous about everything, but once we are seasoned we just drive for the most part and give it little conscious thought. We listen to the radio, talk to someone, and think about something going on at work, all the while watching traffic and watching for the next turnoff. Driving a car runs pretty much on automatic.

The real underlying kernel of all this is this simple ✓ thing: Jesus didn't come into the earth to establish the Christian religion, the Catholic Church, or the Protestant Reformation. He came to be the total Life in us. And life is just lived, moment-by-moment, in all its reality, tragedy, joys and sadnesses, as real events. We are not in a laboratory, where each step is analyzed and categorized, described and noted; so that when the "experiment" is finished we get the results we were looking for. Life is a very non-lab situation, in which the experiments are not controlled, and often chaos seems to be the rule. But in everything the Master Weaver, with each tiny little thread, is fashioning a Tapestry that tells an eternal story of love and redemption in which we see each of our lives perfectly threaded with all the others and all the others perfectly threaded with ours.

I AM the book. You are the book. The best I can do in communicating that to others is to tell each that we are our own Book, which is, of course, Christ Jesus in us. When I say we each are the book, I am meaning that in each of our worlds, in our personal universe, God speaks the truth of Himself every day in everything that is -- the physical universe as well as the intangible one. In our consciousness, every single day and every single moment, God is testifying of Himself in everything that is. Everything speaks of Him. When we drive our car to work, everything on the way is God speaking and speaks of God.

This is why I cannot make Him to be a systematic theology. He Who made Heaven and Earth cannot be contained in a temple made with hands. Every moment He is new and I am new, and am myself flowing out of His mystery within me. That sounds very religious and mystical but it just means that when I order the Tuesday Special with extra sauce at Cowboy Bob's BBQ Ranch, I am in the heart of God and doing His will.

He IS Himself and fundamentally He IS inscrutable Mystery. We know Him only insofar as He reveals Himself, since we have no means of reaching Him, and we know Him only in and by His Eternal Son, the Lamb, by Whom He reveals Himself as He really is, which is Eternal Love.

The further-on depth of this Eternal Mystery is that finally the mystery of His Eternal Godhead and Son is revealed and manifest in you and me. The "revelation" of

God as the Son of His Love is revealed in completion in you and in me, as ourselves.

We can only find Him in ourselves. If we do not find Him there we cannot find Him anywhere. Even when we think He is up there or over there, we are finding Him where He is – in the depth of our own selves, where He, and we in Him, just are.

Another on God All in all

All in all truly means everything. When we say God is "All in all," we mean He is the ALL in everything that is. The ALL of everything.

It may take quite a struggle sometimes to come to that place in faith. Because the opposite of the vision of God, All in all, is the chaos we see with our eyes and experience in our bodies and souls. And that chaos is what seems to be the real thing, with no visible remedy. Or at least nothing lasting. While putting out one fire, four more flame up, and fifteen more are smoldering getting ready to flame.

And all that, since we can see it, feel it, taste it and hear it, seems far more real as an unending series of insurmountable problems, than could any supposed "invisible" remedy.

This is the land of temptation. Temptation's job is simply to get us to believe in the temporal rather than God. We're an easy mark because we've always believed in the temporal, so it's intimately familiar territory.

But that's the way it starts, this seeing God "All in all." By seeing exactly the opposite, the temporal raising up its head as if it is a power unto itself and daring us to defy it.

I find there comes a decisive moment in every temptation/struggle in faith. It is the moment of declaration of final intent.

You may argue with yourself, God, or your enemy for quite a while. Say this and that about what you will do, think you should do, think you believe, or don't believe.

But grace has brought us there in the first place, and grace leads us to faith as well. Somewhere in the struggle, the faith "moment" comes, and we let issues go and lie down and rest in God.

When we "lie down and rest in God" (by faith seeing God working all things according to His purposes), then comes the resurrection, which is the Proactive God as Christ bursting onto the scene of our universe, not as a merely passive spectator but as a purposed redeemer, healer and reconciler, the authoritative Word of God. And that spoken Word that is our lives is then out-breathed into our world, and the Spirit changes the universe after the image God ordains by us.

And all of it -- from initially seeing the opposite, to the reconciliation of all things -- is God All in all.

Time

To grab hold of time is like trying to catch up to a merry-go-round, or snatching a sock out of a spinning washer.

We cannot identify any particular moment as "this moment," because the "moment" we think about it, it is already past.

The only reality is the present moment, but if you think of that only physically, then it is something that has no existence. The "present moment" is always dynamic, changing, moving, expanding, retreating, and resting. It is never something you can catch and put in a bottle and then take it out next year and it will still feel and smell and look the same. That's why you have to smell the roses when they're blooming.

In the physical I have the sense of racing against time. I am such and such an age; therefore I am this or that. I have this much time to do that or this. When I was twenty or so I knew I was mortal, sort of, but death seemed an infinity away. Now a very quick thirty-plus years later, experience-laden but hardly a stitch wiser, mortality pulls on every nerve. Time and mortality are really one thing, aren't they? Time testifies to an end to things, and mortality is its most potent brother.

Ah, but just here the Loving Father has another of His jokes, because time, in which all the sorrow resides, is suddenly found to be no more,[88] and mortality is swallowed up of life.[89]

I always thought there would be some great cataclysm before that would happen. Perhaps one day there will be a great gigantic for-all-to-see event, which will reveal that to all the universe. In fact, I'm absolutely certain that there will be. But right now what I'm talking about is in the silence of hearts, with little fanfare, no big parades through town. Just the flood of light from God within the depths of our hearts, Who inundates us in silent awe, the indescribable One Who is beyond ourselves but more ourselves than we know ourselves to be.

(In other words, ONLY GOD is conscious of the fullness of who we are and the "fullness" of ourselves, which is why our life is "hid with Christ in God." In every way imaginable and in the strongest language possible I can muster up, I mean to say that God the Father is Himself as Jesus Christ, Who in His death and resurrection has taken residence within us to be one person with you and me. There is only One Person revealing Himself as Love completely through an unnumbered multitude of creatures who testify of and demonstrate His Love. And we are those creatures, who all reflect as an image the Same One Person.[90])

Again, grabbing onto time as our reality is like trying to grab a sock out of a spinning washer. Chances are, if you manage to grab onto anything at all, you'll wrench your arm out of joint, or worse, get it caught in the spin.

People think God is not real and time is, but it is just the opposite. Time is the most fleeting thing there is -- in fact "it" isn't even a "thing." It's like a revolving door, which never stops. It never arrives. Time really never truly is.

So part of our training as sons of God is to learn to let go of time and everything about it, and to live in God who is both in time and not in time. (Of course, we don't "train ourselves" in this. It just happens in God's always unique-for-everybody training program.)

One of the advantages about the fact that time is somewhat indefinable and hard to pin down, is that the future is wide open.

But a disadvantage of time is that we think we are mired by the past. What has been must continue to be, is an oft-heard litany. You can't change. Your ship sailed long ago, and you missed it.

But in Him we live outside of time and only "affected" by the God milieu. And that means that the past is in God, and the future is in God. That makes God the Living Reality of this current moment, and the past is Alpha and the future Omega.

And in the present moment is the Logos, the *"Thou art my son, this day have I begotten thee,"* and this moment is God in His fullness. God is speaking, this moment, the Son, Who is Christ in You and Me.

In His Death and Resurrection He has come to live and walk in you and me and in so doing He is the light of the world and the salt of the earth. In us.

He walks outside of time in you and me, but in us He experiences time and all its futility, stress and sorrow. In us He reconciles the world to Himself. In us He fulfills His sufferings as well as His resurrection.

You don't have to do a thing but at some point say, "Here am I, Lord, send me."[91] He does the rest.

Believe me. He does the rest. *"Follow me, and I will make you fishers of men."*[92]

There really aren't that many bells and whistles along the way to tell us we're on the right path. There are wonderful assurances here and there, but they are soon forgotten, as the desert gets dry again.

There are no criteria other than Hebrews 11:6 -- *"He that cometh to God must believe that He is and that he is a rewarder of them that diligently seek Him."* Eventually we realize we cannot do even that – in fact believing God is much harder than keeping the Law – and in that giving up completely we find out it is even His faith that sustains us.

Anybody who gets through the desert alive knows that we are speaking of the Living Person here, no figment of anybody's imagination and no boxed-up theological list of attributes. He is the God of the Living -- the God of Abraham, Isaac, and Jacob -- the God of the Desert.

Abraham, Isaac, and Jacob didn't do anything more in their lives than a little farming, sheep and cattle raising, and raising families. They were not heads of state, famous athletes, writers, rock stars, scientists, actors, doctors, etc. Most of their lives were spent doing very mundane things. They weren't even preachers or ministers. They wouldn't be famous or significant in any way in our modern world.

Yet the foundation of our faith is owed to them. Simple desert-nomads, who never wrote any books (not even a "Bible" book), made any cassette tapes, shot no video. Had no website.

How could the "faith-foundation" of the whole world be laid at the feet of a wandering desert pilgrim who never did a miracle, never changed any water to wine, never healed a sick person, never really did anything particularly exceptional except "believe" in an invisible intangible unproveable "God"?

Because that is exactly the point -- Abraham didn't do anything particularly "spectacular." He just *"believed in the Lord."*

For Abraham, to *"believe in the Lord"* was all pervasive.

As it is for us. To *"believe in the Lord"* means that God Himself has brought about all and upholds all and has given His own Son to be the substance of this present moment – in us and in all things.

And here in this present moment is the liberty of time. Because out of the Spirit we speak the word of God as God's reality breathed into this world of time.

In plain language I simply mean that God speaks out of His infinite Freedom within us the ongoing Life of the universe. The free-substance of God awaits our command, our word, and our committal, to begin forming itself into the reality we step into each successive moment.

Imagine that in your refrigerator and kitchen you have all sorts of things stored. You think, "I'll make spaghetti tonight since I have all the ingredients here." That's your "word" as the god of your kitchen. So after a time, spaghetti, garlic bread and salad appear on the supper table, and everybody sits down to a big feast. Everything is like that.

Now time has become the servant. Before it was an enemy in our thinking. But now time is the clear path through which flows the river of God.

I live in time not to be mastered by it, afraid of it, cowering before it, but to clear my portion of the trail for this city of God we're all working on. Somehow there is a flow of God's anointed time from the antiquity of this world and from father Abraham, directly out of his spiritual loins and spilling into the womb of Christ in me. As Christ is birthed in me that time-flow continues, and it is now the time-flow of God spilling out into MY time, my universe, reconciling all those God gives me, and all is God-time, Spirit-permeated time.

   "THIS is the day the Lord has made."[93]

   That is absolutely literally true. THIS is the day.

   The Lord has made THIS day.

   Let us rejoice in it and be glad.

   And know that our *"times are in His hand."*[94]

That Which We Have Seen and Heard

1 John 1:

1 That which was from the beginning, which we have heard, which we have seen with our eyes, which we have looked upon, and our hands have handled, of the Word of life;

2 (For the life was manifested, and we have seen it, and bear witness, and show unto you that eternal life, which was with the Father, and was manifested unto us;)

3 That which we have seen and heard declare we unto you, that ye also may have fellowship with us: and truly our fellowship is with the Father, and with his Son Jesus Christ.

4 And these things write we unto you, that your joy may be full.

The night God finally broke me to mush in my struggle with who Jesus was, I cried, I blurted out, I yelled, all into a silent non-answering frigid-cold night sky. It was December 25, 1972, and I'd had a bad day, topped off with "accepting Jesus" over the phone, along with my wife, Janis, on the extension. We were led in the "sinner's prayer" by our friend Cary, who had called from twenty-five hundred miles away in Monterey, California.

My reaction to having prayed with Cary over the phone was morbid. Some corner I knew had been turned, but I felt like I had died. I felt like I'd given up and lost and I felt like mourning. I had been dealing with "who Jesus was" for several intense months by then. I was an ardent student/practitioner of Zen and some Yoga, but weighed down so heavily with the question of who Jesus was that I couldn't get it off my mind.

I had started reading the New Testament but I understood none of it and it confounded me. I'd spent hours in the past arguing with people that the Bible was just a book like any other and kept telling myself that, but the Gospels greatly troubled me once I read them for myself. But I just couldn't cross certain intellectual bridges to become a Christian.

I think the thing that gave me the most trouble was the idea or concept of grace. I could not fathom that it was that easy. Pray a little prayer and all your karmic debt is erased and you get off the wheel of life and go to the highest heaven when you die. (I thought in those terms then.) And you don't do anything. Don't have to do meditation, do yoga exercises, control your thoughts, your appetites, eat correctly, etc. Just believe in Jesus.

I just couldn't believe you didn't have to do anything to get it.

But "it" just wouldn't leave me alone. God would chase me down streets and back alleys, meet me where I least expected Him, reminding me that He was around. He would press me Himself through a thousand different witnesses who didn't know each other and were often not even the same species or even life forms. Each "witness" seemed to be operating under one divine edict common to them all: to reveal big or tiny portions of the truth of the Living God to me, and to one by one chase me into a corner until they had me sealed off with no way of escape. (God is good at that.)

And that was what had happened that day, Christmas Day, 1972. The hunter had killed his prey, taken it home in his bag, but this hunted still lived, feeling the pain of his death, relieved that the chase was over, but not yet pleased with losing.

I had a makeshift "zendo" (place of Zen meditation) in a little tent I'd made in our hall closet, suspended from the clothes rod. It was such a nice place, a calm place, quiet, untouched by the world outside it. I would go into the little tent, 20-40 minutes at a time, time myself by an incense stick, and practice zazen (Zen meditation: lotus position, hands serenely folded in the lap) for the allotted time. I loved it. I felt cleaner, purer, pleased with myself, just a bit more spiritual every time I did it. I felt like I was getting somewhere, doing something about my life.

Until Cary called us and made us say that darn prayer. Now everything was all screwed up. So I took a knife and cut down my little hall-closet-zendo-tent, sat on the top of it for a while, and mourned and felt sorry for myself some more. I felt like everything I knew before was gone in one fell swoop, and there was nothing to replace it.

Janis found me there and I told her I was going outside. We lived in the most wonderful place then, in a little stone house out in the country outside Rome, Georgia, on top of a hill surrounded by pastures and fields, with other forested hills and low mountains beyond. Houses have since been built in those fields, but back then there were no houses for quite a ways below our house on the dirt road. I left the house and went walking downhill toward a clearing a couple hundred yards away.

It was crisp, cold and clear, the stars as real and as close as the rocks and crunchy red dirt below my feet. I walked down the road to a place where one could see no houses, out of the light, to the top of a cleared field that sloped downward to a line of trees below.

When I stopped and looked up at the sky filled with stars, everything came crashing in on me, and I broke down. I yelled, I screamed, I questioned, I confessed my ignorance, my stupidity -- the nerve of me, thinking I knew anything about God -- because now I knew I didn't know anything, and there was no way I could know and how could I go on and what could I do?

All this I'm yelling out into the night sky which I'm thinking must somehow contain God, though every theory, theology, idea and understanding I ever thought I had about spiritual things went tumbling away into nothing, and as far as I was concerned God was a great big nothing. I told Him I didn't know what to believe, didn't understand about this Jesus, and didn't get it about heaven and hell and the devil. Finally I said to the silent night sky, "If you'll show me the Truth, even if it's Jesus" (I had a BIG intellectual problem with that), "I'll follow you!"

I did not hear a voice. Neither audible nor inaudible. I didn't have any particular "feeling" at that moment. I don't remember a thunderclap or bells ringing or any other thing happening just then to seal the moment in my head. An incredible calm and peace simply settled over me.

I just know that when I came back in Janis could tell instantly that I was different from when I had left. Earlier in the day we had together recited the sinner's prayer, but it was rote in my head, spoken somehow with "will," but with no intellectual conviction. When I railed at God that night, my mind did not believe and I told him so.

When I came back in I told Janis and the others who were there that night, that I could not explain what had happened to me, and I didn't know why, but from now on I knew that I was following Jesus, whatever that meant.

Something had "clicked on" in my heart, and somehow from the heart the choice had come, and without even knowing what I was doing -- without even any mental shift in "believing" -- I knew my path in life from there on out was to follow Jesus. I didn't even know what that meant. I don't know when the shift came. I just know that from the time it took to walk up the hill to the house, I had moved from, "Whatever you show me I'll do," to, "I'm following Jesus." That's as far as I knew.

Jesus had apparently come through the gas station where I worked and after the fill-up had looked at me through the driver's side window and said, "Follow me, and I'll make you a fisher of men." Without even knowing I was responding, I found myself running down the street yelling at him to wait for me.

A lot has happened since then, and I won't go over all that right now, but this is where the 1 John passage comes in.

John first starts out by talking about how he is witness to the physical Jesus. He touched Him, heard His voice, felt His hands, and had lain on His breast at the Last Supper. John was perhaps more physically intimate with Jesus than anyone else. If anyone knew "Christ after the flesh," it was John.

Obviously, however, John is describing being witness to something far deeper than the normal presence of a man as we understand it. John has seen Him Who is *from the beginning.* In other words, in the man Jesus, John has seen The One Who is the Source of All, the Alpha of all existence and being. The Mystery in person. He Who has always been. And that this same Man who is "from the beginning" is also, this Living Man that John witnesses to, the "*Word of Life.*"

The "*Word of Life.*" There has been no group of disciples, ever, more lacking in knowledge and understanding than the ragtag crew Jesus chose. From day one they didn't have a clue. Not to the real stuff anyway, though little by little some of it seeped in. Jesus didn't hook them by His deep teaching. Some of them started following Him before they heard a word. Whenever He spoke, they didn't get it anyway. He didn't hook them by His mighty works, either, though undoubtedly they might've been the first attraction for some.

Without a doubt this is what happened: when He spoke to each of them, one by one, in a place within each which is beyond our understanding and our emotions, the Spirit stirred an unfathomable Love. It had nothing to do with how He looked, what kind of clothes He was wearing, or how He cut His hair. It had nothing to do with His accent or His color or who were His mother and His father. Something cut each one to the quick in his deepest intimate place, and one by one they were undone in the purity of His Love, in which there was no dishonesty at all. In Him they were created; in Him they could find their own lives; out of Him poured forgiveness and peace with God. Their own shame about themselves and the mess they had made of their lives was swallowed up in His lack of shame for them and His redemption of all that had been destroyed and wasted, culminating in their complete acceptance in Him in love. Here in this MAN was the resounding eternal Word of God coming forth to Life, but not just Life in Himself and for Himself, but Life which creates and builds, by going out of itself to edify and lift up the whole creation, filling it with the glory of God, and blessing it with freedom.

Simply put, He loved them. And simply put, they loved Him back. This Life is God in our hearts in love. Period.

As the song "Hokey Pokey" says, "That's what it's all about."

In the second verse, John turns the focus from his experience of the physical Jesus and says now, *"[I] show unto you that eternal life, which was with the Father, and was manifested unto us."*

How? How is John now "showing" to his readers this eternal life?

The life of Jesus was now embodied physically in him, in John. John the witness doesn't just mean he tells what he has seen and heard as a bystander, but rather what he has seen and heard as a participant. John can be the witness because the same Life that manifested in Jesus is now showing up in him. John the witness means John the incarnation of Christ. Christ "formed in" John.[95]

Because He commanded us to eat His flesh and drink His blood we don't get off the hook by getting to just be a bystander, someone who just sees things from afar. We are now here as participants in the heavenly kingdom, which means God lives in us as His temple, and being partakers of His Body and Blood, we find ourselves in the fellowship of the Father and the Son.

That doesn't mean some big religious extravaganza. It simply means we are in the fellowship of His sufferings and our lives are given for the life of the world, which is what to be "in Christ" means. It is a fellowship of love, which is the only glue that holds it together.

And just here is the point I am making.

John, as did Paul, did not bring them a message written on tables of stone, or written on paper made from wood, but instead a living message, written on the fleshly tables of the heart -- in the human person. John came AS the message, a living human person. He is God of the Living, not the dead. We ARE the message! The messenger is the message. The Living Christ is not the object of doctrinal debates, but a Living Person Who has His fan in His hand, and will burn up the chaff with unquenchable fire. When He comes into His kingdom He burns off everything that is not of Himself. And what is left is Christ only. And that "burning" is what takes place within us.

That Christmas night it was just the sky and me. Nobody else. It was too much for me, and I had to repent in my heart of thinking I was somehow God. I didn't know then that was what I was repenting of, but it was. That night I couldn't put my finger on what happened. But today I have some understanding.

That which was from the beginning, which we have seen and heard, declare we unto you.

I did not have even the tiniest "vision," or any other kind of verifiable spiritual experience. I did however see Him Who is from the beginning. There is no explaining how. I had no knowledge, no understanding, not one memorized scripture, except maybe John 3:16, and for the most part at that moment I didn't have one intellectual agreement with any tenant of the Christian faith, not one, except maybe that I suspected there might be a God. (And I was by no means certain of that.)

But despite that, as Abraham found righteousness in God without being circumcised, I knew the One Who IS from the beginning in the grace I found to believe that night, without any further or improved knowledge of Him. The dark night that had become my life changed in a moment, or at least in the time it took me to walk in from the dark, into the dawn of a Day I had never imagined.

I didn't know a thing. Not one blessed thing about the "Christian life." Oh, but I had found HIM whom my soul so desired (without ever realizing it)! I walked into that house that night "knowing" God. Or rather, "known of Him."

Now it's been more than a few years since that day. And today I "know" a whole lot more. I know scriptures galore, have sat through hours and hours of teachings and sermons. I've been to numerous weekend conferences, read book after book, have devoured the Bible (at times, and at other times avoided it), have had more spiritual discussions than any man needs, but I'm sure that on the official "Percentage of God-knowledge Scale," that I haven't moved up too far from where I started. I've at best only cracked into the outermost layer of the shell. I marvel every day at how little I know.

But I know this pretty well. We declare what we have seen and heard. What we have seen and heard is what we have lived, what we have known within, what has welled up inside us as the Living Truth, which could not be contained, nor fully explained, and certainly not predicted. But which nonetheless had to go out, because if we would not cry out, *"Blessed is He Who comes in the Name of the Lord,"* then the rocks would testify in our stead.

That first night I came in from the bitter cold and declared Jesus the Lord. There were four other people there that night, besides Janis. One of them knew Jesus within the week. Two more within three months. The last one a year later. Love flows out. All on its (HIS) own!

If you have received Him then whether you know it or not your life is the outflowing life of the Living God in your world -- with no effort, planning, scheming, etc., required on your part. He does hidden miracles every step you take, because you are His temple where He has taken up residence in liberty and love by hiding the limitless fullness of Himself in your weak frail human frame.

Things That Go Creak In The Night

"Things that go creak in the night." You know what I mean. Scary things. One of the most frightening experiences I had as a child was one particular time camping in the woods. The Boys Club in Rome, Georgia, sponsored Camp Glen-Holla, where we young boys would spend one or two grueling weeks each summer being run through the paces in activity after activity, all day long, so much fun you couldn't stand it anymore.

There was a camp store where everybody bought honey buns and cokes. I liked archery, fishing, and boating the best, arts and crafts the least. I learned the song, "Ninety-nine Bottles of Beer on the Wall," while we all rode in the camp bus to the swimming pool in downtown Rome.

There were only COLD showers, and our counselors would march us down to the showers every night, in our skivvies (white jockey underwear), carrying our towel and soap dish, and if we wouldn't strip and jump into the shower by ourselves, they'd make sure we got a shower anyway by tossing us in. They tossed me in at least once.

The big finale night there was of course an "Indian" ceremony -- these were not politically correct times -- where we would be "braves" and do some sort of play around a campfire while our parents watched from the hill above and cracked jokes with each other.

The "scary" thing, however, had occurred on our campout a few nights before the finale. They went all out for the campout. They gave us a packed lunch, and the counselors marched several groups of us en masse into the deep woods a couple of miles from the campgrounds, carrying our sleeping bags, flashlights, and sack lunches, which were to be our evening meals once we'd settled in.

After we had eaten and scoured the woods for firewood and we all felt very important and awed by the pine forest and proud of ourselves for being there, the counselors got us into our sleeping bags all around the campfire. Slowly we began to relax under the pines with the clear sky peeking through the branches above. Even in the little peeks through the branches, we were touched with the blazing stars that were just as compelling and mysterious as the campfire.

It's one of my first memories of the warmth and safety of a campfire, being in the strobe-like effect of its light, with its smoke and shifting shadows rising in the trees and up through the branches into the blackness above. I was lost in a reverie of the fire and forest when the counselors started telling stories. Of course they told ghost stories, because that's what you do with young boys on campouts. Try to scare the wits out of 'em. Don't know why, but that's what people do. But it wasn't the ghost stories I remember from that night, nor is it what frightened me so badly.

One of the counselors started telling the story of Jesus coming back in God's wrath. Now I had a child's understanding and belief in God then. It wasn't until much later that I came to a conscious knowing of Jesus as my Savior, but I can't say I didn't believe when I was a child. God was always part of my environment. My mother had read a book about God to me as a small child. I remember the book and especially one particular picture in it. It was a landscape with the sun shining brightly in back of it, and the landscape was lush and plenteous and everything looked full of light and abundant. In my child's mind I took that picture into myself and associated it with God. It was a picture of peace and comfort and I didn't know any other until much later.

This was another picture of God that came that night. This fellow talked about how angry God was with everybody. How He was going to come in the clouds, and how He was going to punish all the sinners, which apparently was everybody, and He was going to **BURN** them up with an unquenchable fire. I don't know how long he went on. But he certainly had our rapt attention. Some of us were from churches that didn't talk about stuff like that, and this was way different from the ghost stories. Ghost stories were fun, and it was fun to be scared by them.

But this wasn't fun, because he was talking about something absolutely real that he convinced us could happen any moment! I suppose he must've talked about folks getting saved, but oddly I don't remember that. I just remember hearing about the anger, the wrath, the punishment, and especially the fire. Just before story-time the campfire, by its light and heat, had sent me into a peaceful boyish meditation, but now by this counselor's story, that same fire had become now a raging inferno of pain, violent anger and suffering.

The sky above me changed that night from a sky blazing with blessing and light flowing out of every dark cranny, into a panorama of terrorizing fear. It had become the scene where any moment could witness the descent of unbridled wrath, and the punishing and consuming fire of the angry Jesus.

So that night I lay awake nearly until the dawn, trembling, afraid to go to sleep, thinking any moment

Jesus was going to come, and was going to burn me up along with everything and everybody else.

It was a childish thing, but I had had a childlike love and trust in God, and then fear came and changed the very sky and the stars. God became different then. And I felt my nakedness and was afraid.

That lasted a very long time, years and years. Even long into the years after I came to know Jesus. I felt I was naked and I was afraid. It got so bad I would physically jump when the phone rang. I knew it would be bad news. It often was.

I began to think my life was a house of cards that could come tumbling down any second, and then everybody would know, everybody would see, what an idiot I've been, how foolish, how unwise, how this, how that. Always barely averting catastrophe, somehow keeping afloat, afraid of the next letter in the mail, laughing to keep from crying, tragedy, woe, bad luck, poor judgment, not enough umph, too much this, not enough that, you name it, if it's wrong or a sign of failure or faulty character, I've been down its road. I've smelled its smell.

According to your faith be it unto you -- and fear was my faith and fear wreaks havoc. It makes its own body.

Does anybody know that this makes no difference whatsover to God?

What do you mean?

I mean simply that in a moment, in a twinkling of an eye, we see the truth, and it does not matter one whit what was past, or what might be tomorrow, and in seeing the truth, all the old spells are broken, fear which hath torment is dissipated, and the habitual anticipation of evil and the expectation of its sure and certain consequences become as something we can't remember anymore.

He Who Causes To Be, Whose name is I AM, is all there is and He is nothing but unbounded goodness toward us forever.

"Let us therefore come boldly before the throne of grace."[96]

What is this? Where is the "fear" in this love?

We are <u>invited</u> to come <u>boldly</u>, which means with <u>confidence</u>, not with downcast eyes or with feigned unworthiness! When we are invited to participate <u>boldly</u> we are considered as equals, as sons of the house, heirs of all the Father's goods, with a right and a say in the distribution of all those goods!

And the answer, when we come boldly -- is <u>grace</u>! More than we asked! More than has entered into our minds! More than we have seen!!!! An answer before a call!!!! A supply already before things start running out!!!!

Awake thou that sleepest, and Christ shall give thee light![97]
O ye of little faith, wherefore did you doubt?[98]

In a moment, in a twinkling of an eye, we are changed. We step into a new land. A new country. And the way of life is different in the new country.

The landscape before us changes from one of fear and anticipation of the worst, to a truthful apprehension of the unalterable fact that blessing flows from out of God within ourselves into the world, and we thus change the world, by being its light and its salt, as Jesus said we are.

You change the world (from a cursed place to a blessed place) by your presence, which is God Present. You change it by your word, which is His Word by you. And you change it by your life, which is given for the world, even as His was.

"I will lay me down and sleep, in peace, for thou O Lord, only makest me to dwell in safety."[99]

Can you believe that?

You can rest, for you dwell in safety. There is nothing to fear. *"Fear not, it is I, I AM." "Before Abraham was, I AM."*

You are the salt of the earth. You are the light of the world. Not by your effort.

No, not by any human effort. Not by any human system of thought or set of ideas. Not by many prayers or much study. All that is as dung. Pooh-pooh.

"Fear not, little flock, for it is your Father's good pleasure to GIVE you the kingdom."

You just ARE.

Take that. "In a moment, in a twinkling of an eye, we are changed...."

"But now, O LORD, thou art our father; we are the clay, and thou our potter; and we all are the work of thy hand."[100]

I look out the window now, and I don't imagine suffering and pain coming. The coming of the Lord, *"Maranatha, Come Lord Jesus,"* is now an occasion of joy and revelation. The original landscape has been restored. It was always there, full of light, blessing and hope, the sun shining on a lush garden, full of colors and life, water and earth. Earth teeming with life, filled with heaven.-

God All in all and Choice

Luke 18:18 And a certain ruler asked him, saying, Good Master, what shall I do to inherit eternal life?

19 And Jesus said unto him, Why callest thou me good? none is good, save one, that is, God.

20 Thou knowest the commandments, Do not commit adultery, Do not kill, Do not steal, Do not bear false witness, Honour thy father and thy mother.

21 And he said, All these have I kept from my youth up.

22 Now when Jesus heard these things, he said unto him, Yet lackest thou one thing: sell all that thou hast, and distribute unto the poor, and thou shalt have treasure in heaven: and come, follow me.

23 And when he heard this, he was very sorrowful: for he was very rich.

24 And when Jesus saw that he was very sorrowful, he said, How hardly shall they that have riches enter into the kingdom of God!

25 For it is easier for a camel to go through a needle's eye, than for a rich man to enter into the kingdom of God.

26 And they that heard it said, Who then can be saved?

27 And he said, The things which are impossible with men are possible with God.

Luke 14:33 So likewise, whosoever he be of you that forsaketh not all that he hath, he cannot be my disciple.

The devil said, "I have something that is my own, my own responsibility, my own ability, and I am something because of that. I am all there is. I create and control my own destiny. I make my own choices. I am all there is to myself."

If I say, "If you take responsibility for anything, you must take responsibility for everything," some might hear irresponsibility and passivity and will say, "He's saying, '*Let us sin, that grace may abound.*'"

However, others will understand what comes as a sure knowing from within, that when Jesus says, "*forsaketh all that he hath,*" He means the utmost of all that we are, which in the end is finally and only our sense of self and all that extends from it. Death is sinking down into nothingness and having no more protective-sense of self.

That sounds total, and nihilistic. Yet that is the Cross in its most pervasive act. The enmity was slain in His body on a tree, that is, the "*handwriting of ordinances that was against us, which was contrary to us, and took it out of the way, nailing it to his cross.*"[101]

"*He who loses his life will find it, and he who seeks to save his life will lose it.*"[102]

Jesus has gone as the forerunner for us, as the Captain of our Salvation, holding onto everyone of us who are His sheep, not losing even one of us, and has Himself by the sacrifice of His own body and blood, provided eternal forgiveness and reconciliation to all who will come to the Feast.

"*Ho, every one that thirsteth, come ye to the waters, and he that hath no money; come ye, buy, and eat; yea, come, buy wine and milk without money and without price.*"[103]

Those who have no money, nothing to offer, nothing to add, are those who come to the feast, who drink the heavenly waters, out of whose bellies flow rivers of living water of infinite abundance into the world.

They are those who have lost all because they have seen for themselves: *"Then said I, Woe is me! for I am undone; because I am a man of unclean lips, and I dwell in the midst of a people of unclean lips: for mine eyes have seen the King, the LORD of hosts."*[104]

We are undone. No remnant of who we formerly were remains, and yet we seem the same as we were. Still faith and firm inner knowing witness to the invisible and imperceptible.

This is the entire meaning of Galatians 2:20. We've explained it countless times in a thousand different ways, but it always boils down to -- God does All, and we do nothing.

Those who still have to do something are those who stand before the mountain of the Law like the children of Israel and can't touch it, because they still live in the wrongly responsible self. It imagines itself something, either good and capable of good, or evil and intent on evil, or as is more commonly thought, a mixture of good and evil. But this supposed "self" is none of those, since it is completely false in its inception and is nothing but a will o' the wisp, a non-existent chimera, that dies when it attempts to touch the mountain of God.

"I live yet not I but Christ liveth in me," is total. Absolute.

There is no room in this equation for anybody but Christ.

To try to equivocate and qualify and define and subdivide this equation which has only one answer and one answer only -- "Christ liveth in me" -- is to slip right back into the wrong tree. The wrong tree wants to know

In Eden

who is responsible and what self is "making the choices."

That's the devil's tree. *Knowledge of the Tree of good | Evil*

OR Tree of Life

God's tree has only one answer: God is All in all.

In order to come to that the path is simple: we die with Him in His death, and we rise with Him not of ourselves but wholly by a power and Life not our own but that of Another. But even though by Another (Jesus Christ of Nazareth), it is into a newness of Life which is He living in and as our normal human selves.

You cannot know this except you do His will, which begins with losing all you have. You cannot do this. You cannot do anything. You cannot lose all you have; you cannot become nothing and He all; you cannot forsake father, mother, children, lands; you cannot think it up; you cannot believe correctly enough; you cannot reason it with your mind; you cannot approach unto God in any other way but to believe. No flesh shall approach unto God.

faith "The just shall live by faith"

And finally you can't even believe. He has to do it in us. So we, as do the elders before the throne in the Book of Revelation, cast our crowns before Him and abdicate the kingship of our own lives, eternally praising Him the Source of All, the Ancient of Days, the Lamb Slain from the foundation of the world, and the Water of Life eternally satisfying within us.

We sing with the whole chorus of heaven: *"Thou art worthy, O Lord, to receive glory and honour and power: for thou hast created all things, and for thy pleasure they are and were created."*[105]

Then you know about personal responsibility and choice. Before it's all only self-effort. Which is pooh-pooh, but God is merciful and gracious even toward that. Loving fathers change diapers too.

"*The people that walked in darkness have seen a great light: they that dwell in the land of the shadow of death, upon them hath the light shined.*"[106]

Hallelujah. The kingdoms of the earth have become the kingdoms of our Lord.

To boil all this down is this: get up, walk around, and be Christ in your world. By just being you. You'll be amazed watching yourself be Christ. 1 John 4:17

The Gift is a Gift is a Gift is a Gift

What follows after losing one's life in Christ, is finding it again.

It has been given back, whole and completely new.

You are in utter awe and a state of praise and thanksgiving at the Gift, too wonderful almost to believe, so staggering it breaks your mind to perceive it.

When Jesus declared Himself in his hometown synagogue in Nazareth, it broke their minds and drove them to anger. No one had dared declare Himself the Messiah before. Or at least if some had they'd been proven crazy or deceivers. No Messiah had ever come. Oh sure, they "believed in" the idea of the Messiah. But not a real one, and especially not a real one in Billy Bob that lives down the street.

Here is this carpenter's son telling these folks that the Messiah had COME, and it was HE who was standing before them at that moment.

It was just too good, too real, too right-there-at-that-moment, to be true. Can you imagine going to a Sunday church "All-day-singing and dinner-on-the-grounds," and telling everybody there over fried chicken, green beans, potato salad, home-grown tomatoes and pound cake, that "the Messiah is here, and he, who eateth chicken with thee, is He?"

Yet it was true. Messiah had come, and was standing in their midst. God right there was too much to handle. Most people like God to stay away up in heaven.

Today He has come in you. When He comes He rips apart the veil of the temple. He opens the way into the inmost Heaven of heavens, where God dwells as the fountainhead, out of which pours all.

What He comes to tell you in your heart and in your mind is that death is swallowed up of life and that He has completed by His death the total and complete Resurrection to Life. And He has brought us with Him to the same inmost place where He has gone to reside in the midst of the Throne of the Father. He sits in the midst of the Throne as Lamb and King, and just there in His own bosom we live, too, in the Seat of Mercy, held in the heart of God in love.

When the dawn comes and the first few rays of light with it, it seems to take a long time until that precise moment when direct sunlight suddenly fills the whole countryside all at once. But it comes, and like lightning, suddenly in a moment it is day throughout the whole landscape. Light completely swallows up the dark and you don't see it anymore, anywhere, just in the twinkling of an eye.

This is the Gift He has given in His resurrection. To walk in the Day of the Lord, to be always the forefront of the outpouring of mercy and love from the throne of grace. Not by anything we can do, but by His power and Spirit Who works in us.

When the veil is done away, God is revealed. And the veil <u>has</u> been done away, which means that everywhere we look God is all we see. <u>The Gift is Christ being Himself in our selves.</u> A Gift beyond price, the actual Pearl of Great Price, which we have sold all we had to get, but in the end it was given to us since we couldn't get it by even selling all we had. <u>There was nothing we had that could buy it.</u>

Christ Sold all He had to buy the Church

The Gift is too precious to purchase. There is nothing that could approach its value. It is the Gift of the Life of Christ manifest in our flesh, to live or to die, to be weak or to be strong, to be uneasy with fret, to question, to quiver with anger, to cry tears, to see death swallowed up of Life in every portion of the Universe, in our own private ones as well as the one "out there." The Gift of Life has replaced the kingdom of fear, and grace rules in everything.

To do that -- to believe it and to declare it -- is to do the same He did that morning at Nazareth. It is saying God is right here, right now, right here in this flesh, and that's a little too close for comfort. A little too threatening.

But that is the too-good-to-be-true thing about the veil being done away. This Day God has begotten you His son, to be the Daystar from on High where you live. Messiah is manifest, right now, in this (your) particular flesh.

No one can believe that. One simply can't have a Messiah right here right now. "We KNOW Moses spoke from God (5000 years ago), but we don't know you!"

"*IF ye believed Moses, ye would believe Me.*"[107]

2 Cor 3

"*16 Nevertheless when it shall turn to the Lord, the veil shall be taken away.* More than Savior but our very life.

17 Now the Lord is that Spirit: and where the Spirit of the Lord is, there is liberty.

18 But we all, with open face beholding as in a glass the glory of the Lord, are changed into the same image from glory to glory, even as by the Spirit of the Lord."

The Gift is that all you see is God in Spirit and Liberty, and with open face we look into the mirror to see ourselves but it is Christ who we see in the mirror, and we are finding ourselves changed into the same image from glory to glory, by nothing that we do, but by the Spirit of the Lord.

The Gift is a Gift is a Gift is a Gift.

The veil is done away and we believe, *"Fear not little flock, for it is your Father's Good Pleasure to give you the kingdom."* Because when you have the Father's heart then you know the Father's Love, and in knowing the Father's love, you see how everything from the foundation of the earth has been to give you the Gift of HIS KINGDOM, where only HE who is Love is King. And the kingdom of God isn't something you appropriate once and keep, but something you continously give away (out of an endless supply line) since it can't stay held in your hands anyway but must of itself move on.

The Gift is God in Christ being Himself in this present moment by pure grace as you.

The gift of God is eternal life in Jesus Christ Our Lord (no beginning, no end)

The New Covenant

The Cross is an eternal event, seen in time to our eyes two thousand years ago. But Revelation says the Lamb slain from the foundation of the earth is in the midst of the Throne.[108] All in God is eternal, which is outside of and interpenetrating "time." Therefore the benefits of Calvary have always been available, both pre-Cross and post-Cross, since the Cross in Time is but a picture of what has always been eternally.

Look at 1 Pet 1:10,11:

"10 Of which salvation the prophets have inquired and searched diligently, who prophesied of the grace that should come unto you:

11 Searching what, or what manner of time the Spirit of Christ which was in them did signify, when it testified beforehand the sufferings of Christ, and the glory that should follow."

That is saying that the prophets, whom we consider "Old Testament," spoke by the Spirit of Christ Who was IN THEM[109].

And of course Jesus said, *"Abraham rejoiced to see my day."* Abraham was before the law, so what "covenant" did he walk in? *"The just shall live by faith"* -- the New Covenant (which is really the only covenant). And to prove Abraham "saw" his day, what did Abraham say to Isaac when they were on their way up the mountain of sacrifice?

"And Abraham said, My son, God will provide himself a lamb for a burnt offering: so they went both of them together."

I could go on and on and on with quotes from both the Old and New Testaments, because divine "indwelling" is just as much Truth in what we call the "old" testament as in the "new." Paul makes the argument, in Romans 4 and Galatians, that life in the Spirit has always been what it means to walk with God, and many all over have known this since the dawn of man. He says the "law" or "old covenant" was added because of "transgressions,"[110] because it is the "transgressions" against the law (and the law doesn't even have to be codified and written down, because our inner being has the law of God written in it), which serve to act as a teacher to bring us to Christ, by making us see our guilt and our helplessness.

I want to stress the word "helplessness," because it has never been God's design to make us believe we are worthless scum, because we are not -- even the hairs on our head are precious to Him. (Think on that and take it literally.) The lesson we are to learn is that we are completely helpless to do anything of ourselves.

(People may speak of the "depravity of man," but the "depravity" was never man's, but that of the usurper who ran our show. This is an aside, but what parents would want to impart to their children that they are worthless scum and depraved beyond measure? Certainly we want our children to understand their need of learning, teaching and maturity, but always on the basis that they are precious, and worthy of growing up into fully living adults. Children are diamonds in the rough, as we are in our days when we don't know the Lord, and walk in darkened understanding. But it was by God's design that we should walk there, in order to experience the futility of supposed independence and self-for-self living, and by them

fully experiencing that "negative" we are prepared and fitted to be vessels for full usage by the Father of Spirits.[111])

In our time we lumber over teachings that have come down to us, some of which make it seem as if God did things one way "back then," and in the "now" He does things another way. That was the attitude of the Pharisees. God spoke to Moses, "back then," but they didn't believe in a direct contact with God NOW.

But of course God has always been the same, and walking with Him has always been the same. *("Jesus Christ the same yesterday, today, and forever."[112])* The picture in the Garden of Adam and Eve in their creation starts out with divine life filling the human "clay" and giving it life. The fact that a usurper invaded the clay only submerged the Divine Life deeper into its inner depths, but it didn't kick it out altogether, or man would simply have become an unredeemable devil and been out of reach of God.

Life is now, and always has been, only inner consciousness. There is no other life. Did the "Old Testament Saints" know union with God in a conscious sense? Perhaps some did, I don't know. It is not plainly stated. But what is "grace," except the filling of the Spirit? God cannot impart some "thing" called "grace." He can only give Himself. Grace is God living in and empowering human beings. *"And Noah found grace in the eyes of the Lord."*[113]

Now, we've always been taught that "grace" is "unmerited favor," but that is not by any means the whole picture. "Grace" can only mean a God-empowered life, which means God indwelling and being the Life within the life of the creature.

Look again at Abraham -- *"And Abram believed in the Lord, and it was counted unto him as righteousness."* Paul uses this in Romans Four to prove what we call "justification by faith." But what is "justification by faith"? Is it simply a judicial act, whereby God (way off up in heaven) notes the fact that you have believed in Him, and makes a notation in His "Book of Life," that you are now among the elect? No, hardly! It is not a simple contractual arrangement, where you have filled a part (believing) and God "counts" you righteous, even though you're not actually righteous. NO NO NO NO NO!!!!!

You are "counted" righteous not by some mental acquiescence to a set of doctrinal principles, but because you have <u>RECEIVED HIM</u>, which means (even though we don't know it at the time) that you have received HIM into your heart, which is your innermost self, i.e., your spirit. The "righteousness" isn't some "positional" righteousness, which is not really real, but rather the Presence of God in His Holy Temple, which is YOU, and I! *"The Lord is in His Holy temple, let all the earth keep silence before Him."*[114] (Who is "his holy temple" and who is made of "earth."?)

This is what Abraham did, even though he may not have had an outer consciousness of the fact. When Abraham "believed in the Lord," he received God's Spirit into his inner spirit. He had an "inner" consciousness of the Spirit of God indwelling him, which acted as "grace" in his life to cause him to walk in the ways of God and do God's will. Abraham was a New Testament man, because it is only a New Testament man who can walk in grace! Remember, when Paul quoted *"the just shall live by faith"* he was quoting the "old" testament, an obscure verse in Habbukuk 2:4.

What was "revealed" in the New Testament was what was already foreshadowed in the Old but now made manifest, that ALL men could see from the Day of Pentecost. Because of the Fall, man has thought of God as apart and separate from himself, but He has never been, and can never be. God is not separated from us, except in our consciousness and our faith.

Jesus continually pointed to the "Promise of the Father," which would come after His Resurrection and Ascension. What was that Promise? Peter refers to it in his famous Pentecost sermon: *"And it shall come to pass afterward, that I will pour out my spirit upon all flesh."*[115] His Spirit poured "out upon all flesh" isn't for some big giant whoop and holler rally, but is the demonstation of Christ being incarnated into the entire human family sanctifying all human life!

Perhaps the issue is confused a bit by what Jesus said to the apostles at the last supper. *"Even the Spirit of truth; whom the world cannot receive, because it seeth him not, neither knoweth him: but ye know him; for he dwelleth with you, and shall be in you."*[116] Jesus was speaking of their consciousness, which was about to be changed forever.

Jesus came to demonstrate the truth that God dwelt IN man, Emmanuel, but as I said above, we have all grown up in a consciousness where God is separate and apart from us. The concept of God indwelling man was as foreign to the multitudes of Israel as eating pork. To them, God's "holiness" also meant His absolute transcendence, His complete and total "apartness" from man. The word "holy" means "set apart." So therefore the greatest their outer consciousness could perceive, perhaps even for those who walked in faith, was God being "with" them.

117

But Pentecost broke down the wall of separation forever, as the veil of the Temple was *"rent in twain."* The veil separated the "Holy Place," where regular priests could go and burn incense to the Lord, from the "Holy of Holies," where God's Spirit dwelled in Glory and Fullness, where only the High Priest could go, and that only once a year.

Before the temple veil was torn in two, the highest that man's consciousness had been given up until that point was the "holy place," where we could come, as if apart and separate from God, and offer sacrifices of repentance, praise and worship. The Cross tore the Temple veil in two, divided it asunder, and in Pentecost the effect was finally and fully revealed. *"And I heard a great voice out of heaven saying, Behold, the tabernacle of God is with men, and he will dwell with them, and they shall be his people, and God himself shall be with them, and be their God."*[117]

To go into the "Holy of Holies," meant to be in the presence of God, the actual dwelling place of the Glory of God. Which is a picture of oneness -- union. And what did the High Priest do the one time a year he went into the Holy of Holies? He "interceded" for the people, which is again a picture of being one with God, as Jesus our High Priest *"ever liveth to make intercession for us."*[118] When we are "one" with God, we are joined with Him in His love-flow of intercession for others, the high-priestly life.

Why do I say this is "oneness" with God? Because "flesh" cannot enter into His presence. Only that which is "one" with God can know Him and dwell "in" Him. The regular priests could go and offer sacrifices and burn incense, but they were forbidden to enter the holiest because that is still a picture of separation in our consciousness, apartness from God. God up there, we down here. In union, God's "presence" is mixed with our own, so that our daily living in every activity of life is Christ living.

The High Priest, in going into the Holiest to act as an intercessor, was acting AS God. This is the picture given us on Mount Sinai, even in the very giving of the law. Moses could go up to the mountain, which nobody else could even touch since they would be destroyed if they did, because Moses inwardly knew no separation in his consciousness and faith -- he knew what it meant to walk in grace, in the Spirit, and the intercessory life. Moses was given "union" when he experienced the "burning bush" and was commissioned to go back to deliver his people. Whereas the children of Israel still only knew God as apart and separate from them because they could only relate to Him as approving of or disapproving of them, or as providing for them and meeting their continual self-needs. They only knew themselves "as flesh," trying to keep the law, which of course they could not do. Flesh cannot approach unto God.

So when Jesus said to the apostles that the Holy Spirit was "with them" and would later be "in them," He was not talking about a physical locality, but rather CONSCIOUSNESS. Peter certainly already "knew" the Lord, because Jesus said, *Flesh and blood hath not revealed this unto thee, but my Father which is in heaven.*[119] But Peter's consciousness was still separated, still seeing God up there, he down here, always two. But in Pentecost, oneness is revealed. *I and my Father are One.* The Spirit of God dwells in man, and is the speaker, the doer, the power, the love, the reality of the transcendent Father, in mortal flesh.[120]

That is the New Testament, and is the fulfillment of our sonship in God through Christ. We grow up "into HIM."[121]

All Things New

If, "*Behold I make all things new,*"[122] and, "*new heavens and a new earth,*"[123] are true, then there is nothing that escapes the transformation. "Heavens" and "earth" cover everything.

There comes a moment when we die altogether to this world, and it does not come without a struggle.

When we wake from the sleep of death, it is a wholly new world.

Death has been changed to life. A divine dam has burst, and everything that before had the smell of a pigsty, has been washed clean in the torrent that came down from the Mountain.

What moments before had looked ugly or degraded, cruel, unfair, or unjust we now see in true light – it is all tinged with gold and shining with hidden glory.

The new heavens and the new earth have been eternally cleansed -- which means always -- they always exist in innocence and cleanliness.

The new heavens and new earth permeate all futures and all pasts. Do we understand this? "*For as the lightning cometh out of the east, and shineth even unto the west; so shall also the coming of the Son of man be.*"[124]

Surely this means, and perhaps you have seen it for yourself, that Christ is Eternal, and most specifically "eternal" in us. Our God does not live in our definition of time. And yet the "time" we live in is more "real" than we can possibly imagine. "Time" is an expression of the Living God Who exists "before" Time, and Whose Being and Person give birth to and flow through Time.

The "Son of man," which is Christ residing in us as we living, comes as a flash of lightning which lights up the entire sky at once -- "from the east to the west" -- instantaneously Christ has flooded the whole of the universe with the coming of Himself -- in us. Whatever may happen to a "physical earth" and heaven, the real coming of Christ is within us!

If Christ does not come "within" us, then whatever He does to this "outer" earth is of no concern of ours. If He comes with ten million angels and flashing lights and mighty signs and wonders, we won't recognize Him.

He must die and rise within each of us.

When He does, then you are you, but it is He living in your "you" as "you."

Which makes you totally in your eternal freedom to be completely yourself.

If Christ has set you free -- who is it that seeks to bind you?"

If the Son therefore shall make you free, ye shall be free indeed."[125]

Because it is God Who justifieth. makes righteous

Period.

"Behold, I make all things new."

You can't make this happen, but do you believe God can, and has made it happen in YOU?

Faith is just nodding your head or giving the "OK" sign, or simply saying, "Yes." and Amen

New

What do we think is the meaning of the word "new"? I'm not speaking of an academic meaning, but the meaning behind the word in 2 Corinthians, when Paul says, *"Behold, all things have become new."*[126]

And also, why do we think Jesus said we can't put new wine into old wineskins?

It's because the old has been discarded. What happens to us in Christ Jesus' death and resurrection completely discards the old. What emerges is something totally new.

That's what "new" means. It means it is fresh, unused, without spot, unknown, having no past, because it comes from right now. Freshness and innocence in this very moment, springing out of the eternal.

The old is not even used to put the new into. What was old has been transformed, and no longer exists anymore as it was, and has become something utterly not seen before on the face of the earth or in the heavens.

The old is everything we were, or thought we were, everything we seem to be when we consider our human lives. The old is the "man" or "woman" we have always known ourselves to be. It is what we think of ourselves when we consider our strengths and weaknesses.

That person, who we tend to think of in terms of strengths and weaknesses -- that person -- which is this "false" me -- has been "rubbed out." He is no more. Anything which is of the flesh (and all that is of the flesh) is "poof" -- no more!

We live only from the new birth in Christ. And there is no past there, there is nothing to live down, nothing to live up to, nothing to accuse ourselves of. *"All things have become NEW."* He is new every moment, and doesn't know that former chimera who masqueraded as a person in ourselves. Now that the rightful Lord of the Manor has arrived and taken possession of His Own house that He built, He knows and sees only Himself in us. In being "seen" of God, we live only in His strength swallowing up our weakness, where new wine (His Spirit) has been put into new wineskins (our whole selves – spirit, soul, body), and one not seen by the world ever before rises now as a Son of God, bursting into this present moment out of the cornucopia of plenty which surges out of the presence of God within us.

We <u>are</u> the Presence (not we look for "it"). If we see that for even the slightest moment, the whole universe changes. You no longer "need" anything. *"And he said unto him, Son, thou art ever with me, and all that I have is thine."*[127] And AS the Presence, the plenty of God is moved through us as bounty, blessing, love and grace to the world around us.

Paul said, "Lift up your weak knees" in faith, and to us that means we are no longer all the things that for years have seemingly dammed up our stream -- our lack of dedication, our laziness, our many failures of love, our lack of understanding or our intense desire for others to notice us, to understand us, to know how hard we've tried even though we always seem to be coming up short.

We are no longer that! There is no "inner child" to heal. There are no brain convolutions to unravel. There are no traumas that have scarred us for life. Our human history is <u>not</u> a consideration, except as mined gold!

Jesus passed a man at the pool in the temple area, who had lain 38 years in physical impotency. The man couldn't even drag himself down to the healing pool in time before somebody beat him to it. THIRTY-EIGHT YEARS!

Jesus walked up to him and simply asked him, *"Wilt thou be made whole?"*[128] He didn't ask the man his history, so that He could begin the tedious work of unraveling all the wrong thinking, the sins, and the wrong beliefs that had gotten him into that condition. He just asked one simple question: *"Wilt thou be made whole?"*

All things have become new! You, now (this moment), have a fresh start, for *"Now is the day of salvation!"*[129] Right now!

The "old Fred" that once was, who had his history and knew what he could do and what he couldn't do, has gone away and disappeared into a land as far away as the east is from the west and ne'er more will he be seen. The Son of Righteousness has arisen; the True Lord is in His Holy Temple; the winter is past; the sun melts the ice; the rivers break up; flowers pop out of snow banks; trees bud before their time; the fields are white with the harvest and now is the time to reap.

The Rock of Offense

One of the greatest stumbling blocks in life is that you don't have to do anything, be anything, know anything, say anything, or perform anything, to receive, live in and prove the kingdom of God.

In saying that it doesn't mean that doing, being, knowing, saying, performing, receiving and living aren't going on. It just means that all those things don't get God into us. Those things are rather the product of God expressing Himself out of us.

What did Paul mean when he said to *"put off the old man"* with its lusts, etc., and *"put on the new man,"* or *"put ye on the Lord Jesus Christ?"*

The "old man" is the man of good and evil, the man of attainment. The old man has to know the rules, and lives by cause and effect, and blessings and curses. The old man knows he is rewarded if he does well, and punished if he does not. The old man wants to know which mountain you worship God on, whether in Samaria or in Jerusalem. The old man thinks he can climb up into the kingdom of God by his beliefs, actions, words, and attitudes.

Some think they do things pretty well, but others think they mostly mess up, and generally think they deserve nothing of God. Many think it is possible to arrive at God by good works, good thoughts, right actions and moral behavior, and set about with all their mind and heart to achieve their goal. Still others think living "close" to God requires an excessive amount of devotion not in them, and therefore that condition (of being "close to God") is reserved for that special quality of person that comes along every now and then -- a true saint -- and not for very ordinary everyday people like us.

But also the old man has all his lifetime been in the bondage of the fear of death. For some the actual fear of physical death is with them every day, and for others of us death is more symbolic and slower as its tentacles gradually wind round all the staff of life and eventually choke it out as we persistently deny what is happening to us.

Through the memories and traumas that have beset him all his life, the old man is a man who accuses himself of all the accumulated wrong that has been seen in the world, and the weight of it, even though it is unconscious, is so heavy and the pull of it so strong that there is no way of escape from the drudgery of being the "old man" we've been all our lives.

Even if we have been taught and firmly believe our "old man" is crucified with him, that we are "dead," or even if we have by revelation identified our "old man" as our former union with our old slave-boss, Satan-the-devil, still day after day after day the thinking persists that we are still just ourselves alone and we are the old selves we always thought we were.

When Paul says, *"Put ye on the Lord Jesus Christ,"* he makes the old man null and void. The "old man" doesn't count. He doesn't exist, not even his past. His history does not exist. He never was.

The new man is Christ and the other has gone away.

This man is like a man who walks by a stream in the mountains, who stops and listens to the soft sounds of the water moving over the rocks. He hears the whole symphony of God in the fullness of His Grace in the water, and sees how effortlessly in peace the water moves in an endless flow.

This new man lives in the flow of that water. There is no effort to bring forth God, because the new man finds he himself is brought forth out of the everlasting Spring of God in the upflow of God from His Invisibility to our Visibility. Out of our deep middle flows an everlasting river that comes out of Christ within.

The new man is himself the answer before the question is asked, the reverberation of the Father's Voice speaking "I AM." The new man encompasses the fullness of the Godhead bodily, and moves in grace and peace in the Spirit. He hears behind him and in his ear every moment, "This is the way, walk ye in it," and his very existence is the fulfillment of God's every promise from eternity.

The new man is the tree planted by the water; he is the mustard seed sprouted to full growth; he is the crop of corn that came up: *"For the earth bringeth forth fruit of herself; first the blade, then the ear, after that the full corn in the ear."*[130]

How can this be mine?

Since He is the flow of life in you, coming up out of you like a fountain as it were, then as Paul says, *"the Word is nigh thee,"*[131] and you simply join in with him in agreement. "I live, yet it's not me, but Christ living...."

When Paul says "put off" and "put on" he is speaking of something that is done so easily it is almost not worth mentioning. For which of us, if we are physically capable, think it anything difficult to change our clothes? Unless you're a lady getting ready for a fancy dinner, any of us can change our clothes in just a few minutes. No big deal.

We are tempted daily that we are the old man. With a chuckle and wave of the hand we brush that off. We don't wear that suit anymore. We live from an inner endless Source, and the whole world vibrates in the Symphony of that Source. Instead of seeking blessings and avoiding curses, we ARE the blessings and the blesser, the point of contact with divinity, the outflow of the divine into seeing the world.

And this is not of ourselves, but of the Father Who has called us by name into expression as living wills of God. By His instigation, not ours. (And what He wills, He fulfills.)

A lady told me once a familiar story. She said she got up every morning and prayed, "Now, Lord, I'm giving you this day, trusting that you will have your way in me, and that you will accomplish your will by me today, and that you will bless my family, my job, my car, my dog, etc." Then she said that by the time she'd left for work she'd cussed out her husband, yelled at the kids, kicked the dog, cursed her boss, and where, she asked, did Christ go and what happened to the answer to her prayer?

I am here to tell you that once you ask God to do a thing, it is done and you do not consider it otherwise. Cussed out husbands, yelled at kids, and kicked dogs are the living proof of Isaiah 65:24, *"And it shall come to pass, that before they call, I will answer; and while they are yet speaking, I will hear."* They are the proof that Messiah has come, and that He is here. That He makes darkness to be light all about him. *"Unto the upright there ariseth light in the darkness: he is gracious, and full of compassion, and righteous."*[132]

Beloved, Now Are We

Thoughts that my life could be better or different, if something I had done, said, thought or believed had been different in some nebulous past, are constant. They are almost the norm. In other words, at times my persistent mental state is that something is wrong in the present moment, and it is my fault.

At times in my life I have tried various remedies.

I went through a time before I knew the Lord when meditation seemed to alleviate the condition, because I was certain there would be a progression, and at some point via meditation (and related activities) I would arrive at the experience of kensho, sunyatta, enlightenment, God-consciousness, grace -- whatever you wanted to call it -- and would know all things and be able to solve all my problems. Maybe do some miracles.

I first decided to get serious about looking into those things when I found out I was going to be a father for the first time at age twenty-one. I thought I could maybe accelerate the enlightenment program, meditate a little extra possibly, so I could be enlightened by the time the child was born, and not only find peace, holiness, salvation and enlightenment, but also become a great dad at the same time -- kill two birds with one stone. (Takes most people the bulk of a lifetime, but I was hoping for six to eight months, tops.)

Enlightenment was more elusive than I thought, however. And so was being a great dad.

Here's the thing. In ourselves, the way it's set up to work, we never get to see in the flesh the whole Spirit picture. So it keeps us on edge just a touch, because there is always a sense of not having "attained."

Why? To drive us continually to the Spirit, to continually supplant the visible and temporal with the invisible and Eternal, and to keep the creation hopping by its continual expansion, by means of the conflicts and their resolutions in our lives.

Paul says we remain in hope, but hope that is seen is not hope. If we can see it, then we cannot hope for it. So we still wait with anticipation for the fullness of our redemption. It's the drive whereby we propagate the life, extend the kingdom. For the hope that is not yet fully manifest, for the City still seen in a mist, for the final gathering of all the people of God from the four corners of the earth and all the times of the earth in the best party ever.

[margin note: Israel not the Church]

We see the Beautiful City afar off in the midst, all Complete and Resplendent, but hidden now in the dirt, mire, strife, sweat, blood, hatred, cursing, and wrath that boils and seethes in the earth.

And we still seem like we're a part of all that dirt and mire. At least I do.

Good! We are exactly as we're meant to be.

The Incarnation is God in Christ Jesus "coming down" out of heaven and being one of us. The double-whammy of the Incarnation is His further plan of reproducing the same life in us, so that we ourselves are the sons of God. doing the Father's will, through His Spirit in us. As human beings among humans beings.

And since God had to come "down" out of heaven and be human in Christ Jesus, so do we. We have to be human.

It means we live in and experience the earth, sanctifying it by the Treasure within us.

And to be human means to feel death. It means to feel the quagmire, the catch-22, the contradiction, the fear and the hatred. The futility and the sorrow.

It means touching love in only a transitory way, because sadness can only come from love when love has no continuance, no permanence, and because of that human life has the deepest sadness at its most inner core. Everyone we love ends up in the graveyard.

But there were no cemeteries laid out in Eden.

That's why He was a "man of sorrows." The "curse" in Adam had desecrated the earth, desecrated the temple of God (ourselves), and fear and sin lurked around every corner. He had "compassion on the multitude," for they were as sheep without a shepherd.

But in a miracle now the "man of sorrows" is our inner person, our inner reality, our inner truth! And so in the midst of our peace in Him within, we still find no rest without, because as The Father has laid on Him the iniquity of us all, even so are we taking into our bodies and minds the sufferings and joys of the world we live in and affect.

There is no separation between us and everybody else in the world. Paul says when one member suffers we all suffer. The world suffers, and we in Christ suffer with it and for it. We cannot even leave ourselves out of the guilt of the world. We dare not. If Christ, who sinned not, took the sin of the universe into Himself, and became it, then we, who have most certainly sinned, can only in Him continue His mission of reconciliation as chief sinners among lesser sinners, wounded healers, yet by grace bruised in His purpose.

But the end of it is the reconciliation of all things.

And here's where we have two things always going on at once.

First, all things are already reconciled. That's why we can declare it so in particular situations as we are led by the Spirit, because God's purposes and will from the beginning to the end are already written and already accomplished, and the fullness is in our midst and the incarnation is fully completely NOW.

And the other thing going on is that we still see through a glass darkly, and a city afar off. But that only makes the completion a bit misty to our sight, since certainly completion is no less complete, and perfection is no less perfection.

1 John 3:

2 Beloved, NOW are we the sons of God, and it doth not yet appear what we shall be: but we know that, when he shall appear, we shall be like him; for we shall see him as he is.

3 And every man that hath this hope in him purifieth himself, even as he is pure.

Beloved, NOW ARE WE THE SONS OF GOD! NOW!!!!!

The point isn't whether you feel like it, is it?

He does all. All. If "you" reserve something "you" have to do, you kill the whole grace thing.

Now, that's not a bad thing, reserving something maybe. It takes that, maybe over and over and over and over and over. It took the children of Israel a thousand years or so just to quit following Baal and at least try to keep the temple laws. So if we have a bit of trouble with wanting to do it ourselves for a very long time in our lives, our times aren't in our hands anyway, but in His.

But we are sons who are being trained, and the final training is the course that puts us on the Lord Alone, where there is none but He, and there is no sustenance but He, and there is nothing else. The end result of that "course" is the final annihilation of any sense of <u>self-effort of any kind.</u> The lesson, "*if the Lord does not build the house, they labor in vain that build it,*"[133] has proved to us by many practical lessons that, "*they that wait upon the Lord shall renew their strength, and they shall mount up with wings as eagles.*"[134]

<u>God is actually real!</u> No really, no kidding, I really mean it! And all He does is give, and all we do is receive. God is to us like the sunlight. Just walk outside and you're in it!

This isn't just "belief" we're talking about, or fairy-tales, or religion.

God is actually real. The stories are true. And what it finally all boils down to is that He does and IS it all, and everything that IS, is a manifestation or expression of Him, and does His will accomplishing His purposes.

And grace, which means a life given to us by the Lord Himself and produced in us by God Himself, is available to anyone who hears the call, "*Ho, every one that thirsteth, come ye to the waters, and he that hath no money; come ye, buy, and eat; yea, come, buy wine and milk without money and without price.*"[135]

Get that? You don't bring anything to the table to "buy" the waters and wine and milk of the Lord. Nada. Nothing.

Selah.

The Buck Stops Here

I've always heard that Harry Truman put a sign on his desk that read: "The Buck Stops Here." In a nutshell, that is what God has told us of Himself.

In our human understanding, we wrestle with questions along these lines: how can God allow suffering; how can God allow evil?

Everybody knows the buck stops with God -- whether he "determines" evil, or whether he "allows" evil, or whether he "looks the other way," or however it is we explain or try to get God off the hook when it comes to evil. But bottom line, which of us, when something particularly awful happens, aren't tempted to look to heaven and at the very least say, "How could You have allowed this?"

Because we ascribe to God omnipotence. All powerful. Omniscient. All knowing. We will even go so far as to say He works all things together for good, etc. So therefore, if God is all knowing AND all-powerful, then He could prevent evil. And since He doesn't, whatever the reason, He's the one where the buck stops.

Some will say, "Well, God permits evil because of free will."

Same difference. The buck stops with Him, since He invented free will, knowing what would happen.

But those are all just thoughts of human fancy.

Let's look at the perpetrator for a moment. With this background -- *"God works all things after the counsel of His own will."*[136] And this: *"For the creature was made subject to vanity, not willingly, but by reason of him who hath subjected the same in hope."*[137]

Job is one of the most interesting books in the Bible, and thought by many Bible scholars to be one of the oldest. The most interesting part in the first two chapters, to me, is a twice-repeated scene in heaven where "the Sons of God" are before the throne and Satan is milling about among them. God questions Satan about what he's been up to, and Satan tells him exactly what he's been doing -- walking to and fro in the earth. Unstated was the fact that he was walking to and fro in the earth seeking whom he could devour, as in 1 Pet 5:8,9, but this was not a fact unknown to the Lord. Between the two of them, they both understood what was going on.

Now God, Who we know also is Love, says to Satan, *"Hast thou considered my servant Job?"*[138]

Now, why did God put it just like that? Like I said, He knew what Satan was up to. No mystery there. Satan would love to get his hands on one of God's jewels, like Job, and bring him down. So God, knowing exactly what was in the mind of Satan, offers Job on a silver platter. In other words, it's as if God says to Satan, "Listen, I know you're looking for somebody to destroy and devour, so what about my guy Job?"

God says, "Do what you will to his family and possessions, but don't touch him." God, knowing FULL WELL what Satan would do, i.e. destroy Job's children, his flocks, his business, bring him to ruin, (and remember, Job was considered "upright" by the Lord), gave leave to Satan to do it all. So he did. He killed his kids, destroyed his crops, slaughtered or had all his herds stolen, and brought Job to his knees, saying, *"The Lord giveth, and the Lord taketh away."*[139]

Even though Satan had done this, Job did not ascribe the catastrophe to him, but to the One from whom it had really come, the One where the buck stopped – the one who gave, and the one who took away.

But that wasn't enough. The scene is repeated in chapter two; only this time the Lord gives permission for Satan to touch his body. So God's precious upright servant, who has walked with the Lord and lived justly all his life, at the instigation of God, is mercilessly attacked by a ravaging disease of the skin, so that he has boils all over him, and he is almost brought down to despair. Yet even then he says, *"Though he slay me, yet shall I trust Him."*[140]

Though HE slay me, Job says, referring once again, to God, and not the devil. The devil inflicted the boils, yet Job gives credit where credit is due, for as Jesus said to Pilate, *"Thou couldest have no power at all against me, except it were given thee from above."*[141] Who filled Judas' heart to betray Jesus, and led the temple guard to the Garden of Gethsemane? It was Satan. Yet to whom does Jesus ascribe the power that has brought Him to this point? *"From above."*

Now this is the sense in which we say, "we see only God, and don't see a devil." Not that the devil and his works aren't there, but we see him within the plan and will of God, even while he acts as an adversary. God uses, and not just uses, but actually provokes Satan to his tasks, the ultimate purpose of course being the *"glorious liberty of the sons of God."*[142]

But we might also say, "if we see a devil, then it's only God in devil form." That takes it a step beyond. That sounds out there on the fringes.

It is on the fringes, more exactly on the sharp edge of truth. Because the basic reality of our existence is simply that God is All in all, the Same Person in all, the One True Self in the universe, and that no sentient creature, angel or man, can live except it lives and moves and has its being in Him.

He is the Source out of which all things come, but most especially persons in his image, created to reflect His Person, to mirror Him as the True Source and True Self of which they are but created expressions and forms. When Paul said, *"our life is hid with Christ in God,"* he wasn't just being poetic, but stating a simple truth that Life, Person, Consciousness, Selfhood, ALL these things, are found only in God in Christ. They don't exist outside of Him, for there is nothing outside of Him, since He is before all, through all, and in all.

Everything in the universe exists and is upheld in the Word of God, which is Christ, and "by Him all things consist." Therefore any particular form in any realm in the universe consists in its basis in God, in Christ, upheld and sustained by the Eternal Word of God. That includes any form that is a vessel (container) of honor, or a vessel (container) of dishonor. All are forms of God. All do his will. As Moses did his will, so did Pharaoh.[143] That doesn't excuse Pharaoh from his sins, or Satan.

The reason why this is important is because seeing the devil as who he really is, unmasked, is how we live in fulfillment of the passages from Ephesians & 1 Peter regarding resisting the devil. We "resist the devil" by ascribing to him no power.

"The prince of this world cometh, and he hath nothing in me."[144] *"Give no place to the devil."*[145] What place? We

know in the death and resurrection of Jesus, we have been translated out of the power of darkness into the kingdom of Light. We have passed from Satan unto God.[146] Our "old man" (old union with the god of self-for-self) has been shattered and put in the grave. A new man has arisen, Christ in me, and we can say now, as Jesus said, *"The prince of the this world cometh, and he hath nothing in me."* He has no foothold, no toehold, no hidden bits of territory that are still his, no -- the Lord of Hosts has come to his temple and cast out the moneychangers and thieves, and has turned it into a house of prayer! Therefore we give NO PLACE, anywhere, to the devil. He has no power anywhere! Only God is on the Throne!

Years ago when my children were in elementary school (now I'm a grandpa four times over), a couple of them came home around Halloween time and told me that some kids told them their parents wouldn't allow them to go "trick or treat" because Halloween was the "devil's night." They didn't want their kids participating in "devil worship." I said, "I'm not giving the devil a day," and we let our kids dress up and go out in joy and dress up on Halloween night.

Satan's deceit is to make people think he has a throne of his own, and he is at least as powerful as God, and they live sort of on a fifty-fifty balance. No, there is only one God in the universe, as there is only One Person. And all the "power" is His (because it consists of His "being"). Whatever "power" Satan has at his disposal he has at the discretion of the Almighty, and uses it at the instigation of the Almighty, even though in his self-deceit he thinks he has his own power and does his own deeds.

But the buck stops with God. God's purposes aren't evil, but He uses the agitation of evil, the negativity of evil, to bring about the reconciliation of His universe, and the full manifestation of we His sons in the glorious liberty of the sons of God.

In this way also the sons of God, ourselves, "defeat" the enemy, when we recognize within ourselves only ONE, only One Self, who lives and moves and has His Being in us. It is there, in the oneness of selves within us, in that we are "one spirit" with the Lord, two yet one, one yet two, He in us, we in Him, that is the secret place of the Most High, the bulwark against the ravages of the storms the enemy sends our way. He is our shield and buckler, our Rock of Defence, our high tower.

When you see Satan has no power over you (or ultimately over anything, for that matter), even though he tries to convince you that you are still susceptible to him, you find yourself free to live without fear in the kingdom of God. Because whatever comes your way, or anybody's way, you now see to be meant by God to bring life, even if for the moment it looks like death. *"O death, where is thy victory, O grave, where is thy sting?" "But thanks be to God, which giveth us the victory through our Lord Jesus Christ."*[147]

And further, once seen as the liar he is, all his false works are undone in our word. Everything he said he ruled he is cast out of, and in everything his degradation and waste is undone into purity and life by the word God speaks by you and I.

Exceeding Abundantly Above All We Ask Or Think

"Now unto him that is able to do exceeding abundantly above all that we ask or think, according to the power that worketh in us ..."[148]

It is sometimes easy for us to think of ourselves as dolts, or slow-witted, because it seems to take so long for the reality that we are enveloped in nothing but God's personal love to seep into our settled knowing. It isn't because we are dim-witted that makes it so difficult to believe, but precisely because it continuously has this quality about it, that it is "exceeding abundantly above all that we ask or THINK!" It is exactly that -- His Life in us, as us, is above and beyond, always, whatever we ask and whatever we "think."

It's that "something" you can't quite mentally grasp, because to truly "grasp" the wonder of grace with an unfettered vision of the dynamic force of God's love, would absolutely break our puny minds. We would mentally meltdown and do nothing but babble the rest of our lives. They would put us in the loony bin.

So He mercifully gives us our awakenings in doses we can take. It always has that ring of "too good to be true" to it that makes people who are too careful stay away. Because it IS too good to be true, at least to our mortal minds!

What is too good to be true? That this moment, this instant, this TOO-GOOD-TO-BE-TRUENESS (*above all that we ask or think*) is functioning right now within us *"according to the power that worketh in us."*

What power? The Power of the Living God, the only power that works within us. The Eternal Power, generated by the Spirit who within us every single moment *"maketh intercession for us with groanings that cannot be uttered .... according to the will of God*"[149] In other words, this is going on all the time (or eternally if you prefer) without necessarily our "conscious" involvement -- what LOVE!!!

Can this really be so?

Paul precedes the above part with this: *"That Christ may dwell in your hearts by faith; that ye, being rooted and grounded in love ..."*[150] Therefore dwelling in Him in faith, our root and ground is Love because that is what He is.

Paul goes on: That they ... *"may be able to comprehend with all saints what is the breadth, and length, and depth, and height; And to know the love of Christ, which passeth knowledge, that ye might be filled with all the fullness of God."*[151] To be filled with the fullness of God, to know the breadth, the length, the depths, the height, of HIM, is to know, to be, to live, Love.

This divine love is not just sentimentality or emotion, but a living driving force, a compelling reach to extend and propagate itself by giving birth to itself out of itself, to generate Freedom and Liberty, to express itself in differentiation and to delight in it, to uphold, to build up, to expand in unbounded Liberality, by means of a Lamb slain in the innermost depths of All.

This is the heritage, the inheritance, of the sons of God, a too-good-to-be-true unbounded, unending, indescribable, unbelievable-to-the-mind-of-man no-holds-barred ETERNAL LOVE operating in us, in every facet of us, as us, in every facet as us, around us, in everyone, everywhere.

It's always above all that we ask or think

But nonetheless absolutely unfailingly true.

Son of Man

"Son of Man" is a very pregnant phrase. "Son of God" is a phrase we are more at ease with, theologically. "Son of Man," however, is a little more nebulous to us.

Theologically, Son of God means, obviously, something more universal than God "fathering" a "Son" in the human sense. "Son of God" means the "visible" expression of the eternally invisible God. The "Word" of God. The Expressed God.

That's kind of old hat.

Son of Man, now that's something else besides. First of all, why not "root of man?"

As "Son of God," He is the "root of man." The Source. No need to quote chapter and verse here.

But why, when He comes as Savior, is He "Son of Man?"

Here is how it seems to me. For a couple thousand years people have been pulled off into the theological issues of the divine vs. the human nature of Jesus, missing the really one vital key element of the whole thing. (There were even wars and uprisings over this in ages past -- people have been burned at the stake for having the "wrong answer.")

But it is not about, ultimately, solving that theological debate about how much was Jesus of Nazareth "God," and how much was he "human." "Son of Man" means something much more personal to me. Something that matters to me, more than the intellectually correct answer.

When I consider how Jesus was "born of Mary," and this phrase, "Son of Man," together, it only solidifies again for me the realization that the "kingdom of heaven is within you."

It is the "Son of God" from heaven who comes "down" to deliver and save us. He is the Beyond, the Eternally Other, the Divine Love who appears as Miracle and Grace and Blessing from "beyond" us.

It is the "Son of Man" who rises up as us, living out our human lives, in the totality of our human selves. The "life" that emerges from Galatians 2:20, 2 Corinthians 5:17, etc., is the Son of Man risen in us. Born of man. Living a human life. In other words, God's eternal plan has been MAN, rising up as MAN, and of course, we're talking the "*man in whom the Spirit of God is.*"[152]

"For since by man came death, by man came also the resurrection of the dead. For as in Adam all die, even so in Christ shall all be made alive."[153]

Salvation, (which was lost by man and must be restored within man), i.e. Christ within us, is an <u>entirely inner event</u>. Christ is the *"seed of God"* it says in 1 John. We are the wombs in which the Father plants His seed. When the child is in the womb, no one can see it. Christ "grows up" within us, as the spawn of man, even as Jesus appeared as the spawn of Joseph and Mary.

The angel said to Mary: *"The Holy Ghost shall come upon thee, and the power of the Highest shall overshadow thee: therefore also that holy thing which shall be born of thee shall be called the Son of God."*[154]

God has wonderfully blessed Mary, the Mother of Jesus, as the scriptures attest, but today, we ourselves are in the place of Mary. The Father has placed The Divine Seed within us, and by the gift of faith we open ourselves to receive Him. And just as it was told to Mary, that "holy thing" which shall be born of thee shall be called the Son of God, and that is the hidden life of Christ within us rising up within our very selves.

To really be the Son of God, you have to also be the Son of Man. The Son of God brings many sons to glory. The Son of Man walks with those sons, hearing them, seeing them, being one of them, knowing their pains, feeling their pulls, encompassed with their weaknesses, distraught over their sorrows, gladdened by their joys. The Son of Man learns obedience through the things that he suffers (he learns the "death" of the first Adam). What emerges from our human lives as Christ grows up in us is the Perfect expression of the Son of Man as we ourselves, the sons of men in this world. And that is the Son of God.

When I say an "entirely inner event," I mean just that. (That's all there is.) Christ first comes on our "scene," as the outer or apart-from-us "Son of God," to rescue us from the grips of the enemy of our souls and turn us around toward the Divine. But the Divine Seed grows up within us, imperceptible to us, and what comes forth from His Spirit indwelling our spirit, revealing Himself as One Person with us, is the fully human person we were created from eternity to be, i.e. The Son of Man. The Eternal Living God forever revealing Himself as living "men" (ladies included in that, of course). And that is never perceived outwardly, but only from the Light of the inner man within in our faith.

"And I will give unto thee the keys of the kingdom of heaven: and whatsoever thou shalt bind on earth shall be bound in heaven: and whatsoever thou shalt loose on earth shall be loosed in heaven."[155]

What a commission. What does it mean?

It means, for one thing, that Heaven and earth are in sync. Inner -- heaven, and outer -- earth, are One.

They always are.

As "Son of Man" we stand in the place of the Son in the Trinity, in our human lives, to declare the Word of God. Whatever we say, whatever we declare, whatever we take in faith, received from the Father, becomes our reality both "inwardly" and "outwardly."

By our Word we declare the reality of God the Father. By our Word we declare the Love of God to be going forth from us. By our Word we declare blessing and salvation in our world. That is the place we stand -- to be the speakers of God. Having been "raised together" with Him, we sit with Him at the right hand of the Father, having all authority and dominion over the "earth" we've been given and which we are.

As in Adam all die -- the first Adam, which we were, died in His Cross. The Second Adam, of which we now are, brings the resurrection of the dead, which is first enacted in us and then spoken by us outwardly into the world we live in.

The point is this, I think, in considering the phrase "Son of Man." Salvation, since it was "lost" by man, must be "restored" by man. Man must "find his way" back past the flaming sword that guards Paradise, back to his original innocence (*"except ye become as little children"*[156]), walking in the Garden with the Lord God in the cool of the day. It is with "great tribulation" that we find our way back, as the searing heat of the flaming sword strips us naked again as we were in Paradise, and for us to again enter into that original innocence in which we have no shame for our nakedness. (No more consciousness of "sin." Again

-- "*What things ye loose in heaven, shall be loosed in earth.*"
-- "*According to your faith be it unto you.*")

In the death of Christ within us, the idol we'd built our lives around crashes to the ground and fragments into a million pieces. That idol in which we'd clothed ourselves in falseness, the idol of "me" and "mine." "Salvation" is first of all the destruction of that false god, and then the rising again within us of our true selves, naked before God (having no-thing to hold onto or to "cover ourselves by"), but now we are clothed with His Glory, which He "*had with the Father before the world was.*"[157] Which is the actual "SELF" of GOD!

The old Adam dies, and by man, the Second Adam, the resurrection of the dead occurs, and an entirely new life is born into the world, the Life of the Father, through the Son, expressed by you and by me in the Holy Spirit.

So, the Son of Man is now you and me, and all those in Christ Jesus, walking this world as "*treasure in earthen vessels,*" showing always that the "*excellency of the power is not us, but of God.*"[158]

No longer "Christ after the flesh" means that Jesus of Nazareth is not just an historical figure, whose actions two thousand years ago somehow affected us, but that the Living Christ, the Eternal Jesus (the same yesterday, today, and forever), died and rose again IN US, and we now are the "Son of Man" expressing Him in our world.

Salaam Aleikum

Jacob Boehme, a German mystical writer in the early 1600s, wrote that a true Christian has no sect, and his church is within him wherever he goes. It's always Sunday, and he carries his priest and sacrament within him.

Mohandas Gandhi, in the movie "Gandhi," when rushed by enraged Hindus vehemently shouting about the injustice and violence they had received from rioting Muslims, became agitated with those of his own faith, and told them he was not only a Hindu, but he was also a Muslim, AND a Christian!

A man of God (and I speak without reference to physical gender) walks in the peace of God. The peace of God is the Eternal Presence, which is the center of our Being.

And walking in that "peace" is what Boehme was talking about, and at least in some sense what Gandhi was trying to portray to his followers. The Eternal Internal truly has no sect. It has nothing to do with what church we go to, what our doctrinal positions are, what country we live in, what our political affiliations or opinions are, what we do for a living or how much money we make. It doesn't even have anything to do with what "religion" we belong to.

It simply has to do with one thing, and one thing only. Is the love of God shed abroad in our hearts? (Sort of the James' "faith-without-works-is-dead" thing.)

What are the determining criteria for this?

Jesus was pretty harsh about people professing His name.

"Not every one that saith unto me, Lord, Lord, shall enter into the kingdom of heaven; but he that doeth the will of my Father which is in heaven."[159]

That's pretty harsh, and is somewhat "anti-Pauline" if you get right down to it. He seems to be saying that it matters what we DO.

It does.

We must come to the place where we don't "just" hear the Word of God. We aren't given the Word to just titillate our senses with wonderful ideas and philosophies. We are meant to move into the Word of God (the Living Christ, the Logos, the Universal One, I AM, the Eternal Internal), not just as a nice set of ideas or a belief-system that we have written down in our course syllabus, but as our Living Inward Reality, the actual Sustenance on which we feed every moment of our existence.

Anyone who has ever seriously taken up the quest for the Grail has met the opposing knights along the way. They come riding up around every curve in the trail, arrogantly swaggering their superiority, brandishing their swords, deliciously predicting our defeat.

They seem so incredibly formidable in their battle-scarred armor and mounted on their tall, fierce beasts. No sane person would want to go another step.

But the Quest for the Grail grabs some, and they can't let it go. It's do or die, and though their weapons seem inferior and the enemy before them seems ten times their strength, they ride on into the battle. Victory is not assured beforehand nor is any vision of it clear. The enemy seems to be the one with the overwhelming odds. It looks like all is going to hell before the first swords clash.

In the Arthurian-type tales, it is the inward purity of those on the quest that determines their victory or defeat. But let me leave that for a moment and go back to Jacob Boehme. In the Quest for the Prize as described by Boehme, a Noble Champion appears at the moment of defeat. The battle is all but lost. The soul has been overwhelmed by a foe more powerful than itself. The moment of death is upon it, though it fought valiantly with all its heart and strength.

But suddenly, out of nowhere, rising up in the midst of defeat, the Noble Champion takes up the fight.

The hero is almost always defeated, but somehow at what seems undoubtedly to be the moment of defeat, he gains new strength and is able to strike the fatal blow to the enemy. In the heat of battle, down on the ground, with the enemy standing over him in haughty derision, readying to strike off his head with one more swing of the blade, somehow the hero's hand glances across the sword just within his reach, and in one last desperate attempt to hold onto life he scoops up the blade and surprisingly drives it into the heart of the enemy. He lives to ride another day.

So there is a struggle to attain the Grail. The Grail is the inwardly known and experienced presence. The inward reality of the Christ of God, the Logos, the I AM, the Alpha and Omega, dwelling not in some far off heaven, but eternally in the very center of our own selves.

The enemy is the embodiment of all the reasons and impossible odds in front of us that tell us there is no way we can find our way through the muck and mire of our human lives to find God Who dwells at the ground of our being. We are too distracted by surface fluctuations, so the enemy tells us, or too scarred, or too marred, or too ugly in visage and deportment.

But it is the Noble Champion who takes up the battle. He doesn't come like the Cavalry with bugles blaring and guidons unfurled, but with silence and unseen strength, which has nothing to do with countering the taunts of the enemy, making no attempt to prove him wrong. His accusations are not worth arguing.

When the Noble Champion arises in the substratum of our consciousness, permeating by His presence everything into wholeness, darkness becomes light.

Suddenly we see. The evil knights who opposed us and blocked our way were lying. It had nothing to do with our strength, our purity, or our worthiness. It had nothing to do with how much we fought, how hard we struggled. Because right there before us, right there in our midst, as bright as day IS the Holy Grail.

The Grail is the everlasting source, the cruse of oil that never runs out, the well of water springing up into everlasting Life, the water which quenches your thirst forever, that deep down in the center of your being removes fear from the entire landscape evermore.

The Noble Champion climbs up into us from within us, exuding strength beyond our own, but which we unexpectedly find to be our own anyway, because He has taken residence in us and has donned our form.

And now we get back to the beginning of this. We take God and Christ in the beginning of our faith lives to be our Strength and our Source, with no inkling of where that will lead us.

First it leads us smack-dab into our own inadequacy, our own unworthiness. From there into death and despair. We are undone; we know our integrity is a will 'o' the wisp, ephemeral, and the product of a faulty imagination.

And then there is the Rising. He Who died and rose again, <u>now</u> arises in the very self we had come to hate. A Living Christmas, a Yulelog that never burns out, burning with the fire of unending passion, pours into the whole of our existence, and not just our own existence, but He fills the whole landscape, so that all we see, from the east to the west, north and south, is Christ Himself Who has filled everything.

In that new landscape there are no enemies. Those who claim to be are lying. Those who oppose us really don't. (They only oppose themselves.)

Finding no one to be our enemy, we are free to love unreservedly. We don't have to be on guard, to be wary. (We are, but we aren't.) We are wise as a serpent and harmless as a dove.

When the Divine permeates you, when you recognize Him by faith as ALL in all, then Divine Passion, which seeks only to give life, overtakes you. You live no more to get for yourself, but to give out of yourself. But not out of some fantasy that you have become some sort of wonderful giving person, but out of having found out to the uttermost that you had nothing, and He Who has risen in you is All and has everything. And He has commissioned you to give it all away.

Boehme went on to say that the true Christian, while having no sect, is at home in all of them. He finds God wherever he goes.

Luke 9

51 And it came to pass, when the time was come that he should be received up, he steadfastly set his face to go to Jerusalem,

52 *And sent messengers before his face: and they went, and entered into a village of the Samaritans, to make ready for him.*

53 *And they did not receive him, because his face was as though he would go to Jerusalem.*

54 *And when his disciples James and John saw this, they said, Lord, wilt thou that we command fire to come down from heaven, and consume them, even as Elias did?*

55 *But he turned, and rebuked them, and said, Ye know not what manner of spirit ye are of.*

56 *For the Son of man is not come to destroy men's lives, but to save them.*

For that, you toss out everything. There are no rules in love, except to do whatever it takes to save lives.

"Salaam Aleikum" is Arabic for *"Peace be unto you."*

Which is what our Lord said. Amen. Selah.

The Unlikely and Impossible

Finding God where it seems like God can't possibly be seems to be at least part of our task in this life. And that task, which is finding God in the unlikely and impossible, reconciles the whole world.

He came to be Emmanuel -- God with us -- and seeing the Invisible Father manifest in the Son in the midst of what looks like manure, is the struggle and daily temptation in life.

I admit it, there are times and days I would rather be somewhere other than where I am right now, doing something other than what I'm doing, wishing I was feeling something other than what I am feeling, and maybe more earnestly than anything, I could wish I was a person other than the one I am in this present moment -- a person who doesn't have the life I'm living, who hasn't made the mistakes I've made, who could do this and could accomplish that -- THAT'S the (imaginary) person I'd like to be.

Those are the days and times when spiritual clichés and platitudes -- "God has everything in His hands" -- "everything works together for good" -- can't be functional, can't be true, can't apply to THIS bull-pile right now!

This is the temptation that is common in varying degrees to all of us.

The truth we know inwardly by the Spirit's witness in us to, "*I live yet not I but Christ*," and, "*to live is Christ*," says that we are totally (not partially), He living in us as ourselves, at all times, and that every moment (right now) is the moment of the Lord, and that everything, as we are experiencing being and living in the "right now," is God in perfection. He has brought us (He is responsible for all) to exactly this present moment, to be His presently spoken Word, by the eternal unfolding of His perfect will, expressing Himself perfectly by means of His Sons who have been born again *"unto a lively hope"*[160] in Christ Jesus. Perfect God expressing Himself perfectly through and by means of His perfected adopted sons.

And this is the thing that boggles our minds because we know we are unworthy and stained. Yet we also know that He has put a hot coal from His own altar on our tongue and caused His Spirit to enter into us, and then to stand us upright on our feet beyond the power of our own strength. We were down on the ground without even the strength to look up, and now Someone beyond us has caused to stand.

It's the mind-boggling, head-busting, too-good-to-be-true-but-is-true reality of <u>absolute liberation</u>, to hear and see God the Father above all, and through all, and in all, in the right now, in us in what looks like instance after instance of weakness or failure, of saying the wrong thing, of apparent bad choices, or flawed character – God is All in all in all that!"

No," some will say, "I can't put my weakness, my failure, my wrong unwise choices, and certainly not my flawed character, on God! He isn't responsible for that!"

But God says, *"The former things have passed away,"*[161] and He doesn't remember them anymore, nor do we. We don't think after the flesh. What was former, exists no more except in its real truth in God. The real truth is that all that we were is now redeemed in Him as all meant for good, to save much people alive. Whether good or evil has come our way in the past, whether we have committed

155

heinous sins or been saints, none of it is of any merit (for good or evil) except that God has redeemed us by the blood of Jesus in an eternal sacrifice which has eternal ramifications, eternal effects. When we hear, *"The former things have passed away,"* then we have entered into a new realm where there is only One Tree, the Tree of Life, and the old tree is cut down at the root and put into the fire and burned up. And we feel the burn of it.

In the old tree we trembled and cursed ourselves and others in our vanity and fear and judgment, and heard the howls of the beasts that were after us, and from time to time we joined in.

But in the Tree of Life we have only One Lord and One Who is All in all, the Sufficiency and Power and Wisdom and the Same One Person in us all, and more importantly the Doer of all in us.

The Accuser has only one job. To deny you your sonship by convincing you that you are not worthy of it, and that God will not give it to you because of that. He doesn't work for himself, though he thinks he does.

But from the Eternal you have always had an advocate, a Lamb slain for you, and whose purpose in sending the deceiver, the lying spirit, is to bring forth the Lamb, the Eternal Truth, and not just in heaven, in the Uncreated, but in earth, in you and me.

This is an absolute impossibility for us to do -- to bring forth Christ! People talk all the time about "being like Christ," but imagine the utter impossibility of that! How could anybody even think of it? People backpedal it and say, "Of course we can never really attain it, but we have to try." Why would God lay on us such an IMPOSSIBLE

BURDEN and then call His burden light and His yoke easy? Is He some sort of humorous sadist?

But what is impossible to human ability and infinitely outside the realm of human thought, comes of itself in grace as a gift.

The whole idea of "attaining" unto God is predicated on the original lie that we are selves who could add something onto ourselves -- improvements, enhancements, changes of habits, thought patterns, cultivation of certain emotions, etc. – that would make us "like God." But there is only One True Self, and He by grace Himself in all His created selves, so that it is His love, His power, His wisdom, by which those selves live.

And that why there's a struggle every day, why some days hurt, because we see the inner, we see the truth, which is that God is All in all, and we are His expressions in this world. The "outer" comes to us as opposite, as accusation, as contradiction. Some days the grace doesn't seem to be there and the last thing we want to hear is some cheery voice saying, "Every day with Jesus is sweeter than the day before," because lately and a lot of times it has seemed like, "Every day with Jesus is a bigger drag than before." It's as if we never feel strong, and we never feel quite worthy, and we never feel quite like we measure up, and we honestly wish we were different somehow, or that the Lord would change us into some super spiritual person we know we ought to be and wish to be, but, sadly, He doesn't ever seem to do it.

Then somehow, out of grace from far away, a remembrance occurs, and yes, we remember, and we know that all accusation and contradiction and everything being a big drag was only to see the Lamb in all His glory. All that was only His death and that which lacks of His sufferings manifesting in our mortality, as we fill up that which is behind of the sufferings of Christ in our mortal flesh. It's His Life living in our flesh.

This is the daily cross. To be faced every day with the opposite of the truth, which is just simply that we our just ourselves and we need improvement and we have a whole lot of "oughts" and "shoulds" to get doing in order to grow and mature and to one day (which never comes) reach perfection, rather than the absolute and total truth that THIS DAY IS the reemption of the Lord, whether by my life or by my death. And implicit in being His identity in the world, is to be All that He is, which is to be One with the Father and to absolutely forget ourselves in the liberty of grace. It is to have a baptism of participation in Christ's death for the redemption of the world. And it is to believe an absolute absurdity, starting with believing a man whowas the Son of God rose from the dead, and then to further believe an even more absurd absurdity, that the Spirit of the Father in that same Man Jesus is now in us who are redeemed in His blood, ad that we are One as He and the Father are One, as He prayed for us in John 17.

Every day it look like that is not so. And every day we get to sa it is so.

Let there be light!

In all things

A Little Bit on the Good Samaritan

Normally the story of the Good Samaritan[162] has from our childhood been presented as a moral tale. The focus is on the action of the Samaritan, who showed mercy toward a man who had been beaten and robbed, and then left to die by the side of the road. A story about how one ought to act if one is to be "Christ-like."

But now we consider the wounded man himself.

Do we not realize that just as the Samaritan is Christ, the wounded man is also Christ?

Emmanuel has allowed himself to be disguised under dirt, blood, vomit, and excrement. In Man He has allowed Himself to be wounded, to be stripped of His heavenly raiment by robbers, to bleed naked on the side of the road, to stink, to be repellent and abhorrent to the sight of other men, so that they dare not dirty themselves by touching him and so pass by on the other side of the road.

"Insomuch as ye do unto the least of these my brethren, ye do it unto Me."[163]

When He said that, He was not being figurative. He was being completely literal.

The wounded man, beaten, robbed, disrobed and dying naked by the side of the road, is all of us, the masses of humanity, every man woman and child who is living now, or in the past or future -- Germans, Poles, Russians, Czechs, Japanese, Chinese, Burmese, Arabian, Afghani, Pakistani, English, Iraqi, Persian, French, Italian, Vietnamese, Haitians, Cubans, Mexicans, Africans, Romans, Greeks, Jews, Muslims, Buddhists, Shintos, Republicans, Democrats, Nazis, Communists. And all of that swirling sea of hurting humanity is the wounded Christ, Christ

159

whose heel has been bruised in bringing many sons to glory, Christ Who is the Man of Sorrows, who bears our iniquities in his own body hanging from a Cross, who takes it all into Himself, not figuratively, but literally. It was not by some legal contract -- "If you perform this act, I'll forgive everybody and make everybody who believes a son of God" -- but by virtue of the fact that He is all that we are, by the will of the Father, and thereby is <u>present and living</u> in all the sorrows, hurts, iniquities, hatreds and contradictions of his created sons. He is continually taking them into Himself by means of our lives, and then filling the whole of our earthly existence with Heaven.

So it is then Christ as the Samaritan, Who finds Christ in the wounded man by the side of the road, Who binds up His Wounds and pays the price for His recovery. In both He bears the stink, the revulsion, the sorrow, and the healing. The Samaritan no doubt got the stench of the wounded man on him when he picked him up and took him to the inn. But no matter. It was Christ bearing Christ.

We bear the stench of the earthly. It's a good smell. It has the aroma of life to it. The smell of a farm. There is sweat, pain, sorrow and disappointment, as well as cool breezes in the summer, pleasures and joys, and dreams fulfilled.

To live in the world is to live Christ, which means we are whatever we need to be in order to reveal the Father to others. It means we are wounded, hurt and bleeding sometimes, and other times we pick up the hurt and bleeding and help them on their way.

Either way, we are Christ living. We are the Living Purpose of the Father, a mission of perfect love, which comes from no attainment on our part whatsoever except the grace-given contriteness of heart which says there is only One Will, and that is, "You O God!" By His grace and wisdom He has created us to be living expressions of Himself through no effort on our part to "become something" on our own, in a mystery of union of persons too deep for words.

Pure Religion

"Pure religion and undefiled before God and the Father is this, To visit the fatherless and widows in their affliction, and to keep himself unspotted from the world."[164]

Absolutely everything extraneous is stripped away as the gospel is reduced to one thing only. And that is that we know we love God whom we do not see if we love our brother whom we do see. If there are any litmus tests, that would be the one, and no other.

That strips away knowledge. There is nothing wrong with knowledge. But it has nothing that it can add to love. Little untaught children can love.

That strips away the performing of miracles or other acts of so-called power. It isn't that that those things do not happen; indeed they are to be expected. But healings and miracles do not prove the love nor necessarily exhibit it. Love stands of itself.

Love has many definitions but the best definition for me is, *"love seeketh not its own."*[165]

To "seek its own" is the *"garment spotted by the flesh,"*[166] which we are to hate. Love does not see anything as "its own" (something for "me," "mine"), because love exists only to lift up, to bless and to give, just as the sun exists to give light, and by it life.

Love then is to be as the sun, which as I said above has one purpose, to give light, producing life. The sun doesn't differentiate its shining according to the supposed worthiness of the receiver, but shines freely to all and on all and becomes the life of all, even the life of those who shun its rays, because there is no life on this planet that does not owe the sunlight its origin.

"But ye are not in the flesh, but in the Spirit, if so be that the Spirit of God dwell in you."[167]

Simply put, "in the flesh" means "something in it for me and to heck with you," and "in the Spirit" means "I exist and live for the good of others."

One is the kingdom of the false god, the usurper and deceiver, and the other is the kingdom of the One True God, Who Is All in all, and is all, in you and in me. The liar says The Living God is not All in all, and fragments the world into supposedly conquerable portions that we can have for ourselves. He paints us a picture of us that is altogether false and wholly a lie: he tells us we are whores, liars, bastards, thieves or mistreaters; or conversely, that we are the better than everybody else, we deserve better, and have a right to what others withhold from us. We have no evidence for a long time except to believe what he has told us by the case he builds in our sight and hearing year after year. But it's a desert life and we are always thirsty and hungry.

When we step into the new kingdom and all things are new, there is no gradual improvement, but instead there is an immediate and complete washing away of everything that was past, and by the infusion of the Spirit of God within our spirit to make one new person, we stand up with the exact same "past" as before, but it has now been resurrected and made anew just as we have been, and everything, past, present, future, becomes part of the one Eternal and is as clean, fresh and new as the Eternally Begotten Son is with the dawning of each new day.

"Wilt thou be made whole?"[168] asked Jesus of the man who had been crippled for thirty-eight years. Simple question. First he made an excuse. "Well, sure, I'd love to. But the water is way down there and I can't get there in time; somebody always beats me to it."

But the question Jesus asked bypassed the pool, getting there in time, finding someone to help him down there - all his listed obstacles. Jesus' question cut to the chase: "WILT THOU be made whole?" A yes or no answer is all that is required.

Love bypasses every obstacle and lives in grace. It is a gift and not earned, nor can it be worked up in the flesh. The man has listed all the things he'd "tried" to do and he could not perform well enough to get the healing. Jesus is offering a bypass of the regular way of doing things, bypassing the traditions, and says basically, *"Look, this is a gift being offered to you now, and all I want to know is if you want it or not."* Jesus is offering this man something he hasn't earned *"by the sweat of his brow."* A breakout from the curse of the Fall, right there on the spot. It cost him everything, but the man took it as a gift.

Either we ARE love, which is Christ in us, or we are not His. If we are not love, we are of the wicked one John says.

But to be Who He is means to be What He is, which is Love, and that means that the reality of our lives is fulfilled, the true desires of our hearts are met, when our life is in some measure given away to bring life outside ourselves. There is no other purpose to our living. There is no hope in the world otherwise.

When Paul said, *"I determined not to know anything among you except Jesus Christ and Him crucified,"*[169] he was not making a big important theological statement. He was expressing the center of his life, which was the cross exhibited and lived in love, "to spend and be spent" for others, without regard for his own life.

Now that's the life of all of us in Christ. We exist to lift up, to bless, to testify to the truth, to impart wisdom, and to give life. Therefore as we are loved, we love. As we are comforted, we comfort. As we are blessed, we bless. As we are led, we walk. If we happen to walk into hell, we are not misled. Because we come back out, bringing freed captives and gifts for everyone.

Grace leads us on and will not fail.

"I shall not die, but live, and declare the works of the Lord."[170]

Which Is Easier?

Luke 518 And, behold, men brought in a bed a man which was taken with a palsy: and they sought means to bring him in, and to lay him before him.19 And when they could not find by what way they might bring him in because of the multitude, they went upon the housetop, and let him down through the tiling with his couch into the midst before Jesus.20 And when he saw their faith, he said unto him, Man, thy sins are forgiven thee.21 And the scribes and the Pharisees began to reason, saying, Who is this which speaketh blasphemies? Who can forgive sins, but God alone?22 But when Jesus perceived their thoughts, he answering said unto them, What reason ye in your hearts?23 Whether is easier, to say, Thy sins be forgiven thee; or to say, Rise up and walk?24 But that ye may know that the Son of man hath power upon earth to forgive sins, (he said unto the sick of the palsy,) I say unto thee, Arise, and take up thy couch, and go into thine house.25 And immediately he rose up before them, and took up that whereon he lay, and departed to his own house, glorifying God.

Jesus asked which was easier, to tell someone his sins are forgiven, that the sins are no more and he may give them no more mind, or is it easier to tell him to rise up off his sickbed and he DOES, even though moments before he had been immobile and misshapen? Which is easier, from the depths of truth and love to speak unconditional forgiveness to a person for anything he's ever done or been, giving him a completely clean slate, or to miraculously heal him?

Logic would tell us that healing someone's body by a word or prayer would be a physical impossibility and it would have to be a miracle, something outside the norm of human reality. So that, we would think, would be the harder thing. We don't by and large know how to do miracles. But the first thing, forgiving sins, is even more intangible than doing miracles, and something perhaps more rare in normal experience than we might think.

To prove his point, Jesus did the easier thing -- He healed the man's body.

For a moment consider what is the forgiveness of sins. It is the total clearing away of the cobwebs of the past and present, and an absolute fresh start in the immediate moment. It is an infusion into us of God in His grace, which floods us with divine approval and divine pleasure in us as His sons.

It isn't something legal, like something I have on a piece of paper stating: "Your sins are forgiven." It is instead the inner initial -- and ongoing -- experience with God. In Him we find nothing but blessing, nothing but approval -- even if we have done badly. We may be upbraided for this or for that, but even the upbraiding and trouble for a night turns to joy in the morning, and always does.

The forgiveness of sins is the state of man in the Psalms: *"Blessed is the man unto whom the LORD imputeth not iniquity, and in whose spirit there is no guile."*[171]

The Pharisees were right about one thing: only God can forgive sins.

But what was happening in their midst, that they were completely missing, was that God WAS forgiving sins -- in the person of Jesus.

When Jesus told that man his sins were forgiven, he was declaring something more than an idea or a philosophy.

167

I don't believe Jesus did anything that wasn't absolutely honest. So when Jesus told that man his sins were forgiven, it wasn't just some theological proclamation, some heavenly concept he learned in a book. He was sharing with the man his own inner reality, his own inner truth. In Jesus' spirit, he lived in the Father's forgiveness and grace. The reason Jesus could pronounce to the man his sins were forgiven is because they were forgiven <u>in Him</u>. He spoke truth to the man because it was real in Him! Jesus did not see the man's sins. Instead he saw the cry of his heart.

I don't know any other mission we have in life but to forgive one another and thus to reconcile the world unto God. That is what the Cross did and we are people who are called to live the Cross. The whole human race is called to participate.

Here's the bottom line to me. There is no doubt Christ is the Vine and we are the branches.[172] We are He in the world, whether we like it or not. Now that's a big responsibility!

But like Paul, we have discovered and proved true that, *"Not that we are sufficient of ourselves to think any thing as of ourselves; but our sufficiency is of God."*[173] If we stop right there and consider -- Selah -- "OUR SUFFICIENCY IS OF GOD," then that's a pretty big sufficiency, isn't it?

Now that we see the answer to that foundation question, where our sufficiency comes from, there is no need to consider that anymore, and now that we know the sufficiency, we are the forgiveness of sins and are the reconciliation between God and man, since God Himself IS those things in us! Therefore we are the containers of and manifestors of the Living God Who is in us, and He

IS the forgiveness in us, and IS reconciliation in us, every hour of every day.

But it does cost everything. More than we have. But in a miracle we're given back what we give (ourselves), and the impossible is given out of the invisible, and we are the ones who now forgive sins.

" *To wit, that God was in Christ, reconciling the world unto himself, not imputing their trespasses unto them; and hath committed unto us the word of reconciliation.*"[174]

That means that Jesus is now in you and me pronouncing forgiveness of sins -- which is not so much the audible words but perhaps more so the heart of forgiveness and the heart that does not condemn, and then this forgiveness and no condemnation is extended universally, *"raining on the just and unjust alike."*

Jesus said anybody can love the people who love them back. But Jesus in the Sermon on the Mount said we are to "love our enemies." He wasn't kidding. It is not divine love if it does not love its enemies. Anybody can love his friends, family, and children. Only God can love His enemies. In deed and in truth.

And because that is the Love that is now in us, by grace through faith, the Father says to you and to me, *"Thou art my beloved Son, in whom I am well pleased."*[175]

For All Are Thy Servants

Ps 119:89-91

89 For ever, O LORD, thy word is settled in heaven.

90 Thy faithfullness is unto all generations: thou hast established the earth, and it abideth.

91 They continue this day according to thine ordinances: for all are thy servants.

You find you really do become nothing but prayer.

Back in my beginning days in a Pentecostal church, I heard about "having a burden for souls," and that was up there in my top ten list of the things I wanted the Lord to "give me." Somehow by grace I had found that the topmost was God Himself -- *"as the hart panteth after the waterbrooks, so panteth my soul after thee O God. My soul thirsteth for God, for the living God: when shall I come and appear before God?"*[176] That was, so I thought, something for me, to satisfy "me."

But this other thing, this "burden for souls," well, I didn't know it at the time, but that was for "me," too – to make "me" more spiritual and make "me" closer to God. Of course even through that veil of self it was really the desire of the Spirit welling up in me to form Christ in me and to reproduce Himself and His Life in others by means of "me." But I didn't know that at the time. I thought it was just "me" wanting to improve and get "closer" to God.

My problem at the time was that I was hearing all these testimonies about people getting a "burden for souls," and they would all tell about waking up in the middle of the night, praying with tears for people, or praying and praying for hours and hours until they "got the victory." But that hadn't happened to me, despite the fact that I stayed up late many a night praying for it to happen.

Everybody was especially big on tears. Tears pretty much showed you had the burden.

That kind of "prayer" really never got hold of me. First of all, the other boys had called me "Crybaby!" when I got hurt in football in the 4th grade (age 9), and from that time I had little use for tears. So to develop the quality of crying while praying, at the very least required me trying really hard to work it up. And I tried and tried and tried to become a "prayer warrior" and to "pray without ceasing."

…Change of subject (I'm promised this will resolve at the end).

Much of my life has been determined by the things I have feared. Fears faced usually have brought at least some sort of Waterloo that led hopefully to a good resolution.

Fears not faced usually prolong some situation, often making things seemingly worse by the inertia which accompanies fear, since fear often makes you frozen in your tracks, unable to move as destruction seems headed right down on your head. (Running away is often not a sign of fear, but of good sense.)

Or at least so it would seem. While I might be tempted to think that my life has been "determined by the things I have feared," the scriptures say otherwise. They say in many ways that all my steps are ordered of the Lord, that He has preordained good works for me, and that He has known "me" with infinite "precious" thoughts toward particularly "me." And in a multitude of other ways God lets us know He steps with us, in us and as us in every step we take. There is no separation from Him if He knows us.

People are always wanting me to explain or answer questions about the other side of things. The side where we are hardened toward the Lord, the side where we apparently don't choose to believe. But I don't know that side of things. I don't know what the Pharaohs of the world experience. It is plain in scripture that God hardened Pharaoh's heart to oppose Moses in order to bring about the Exodus, just as it is plain that even though Reuben and all his brothers meant evil in selling Joseph into slavery, still God meant it for good to "save much people alive." Then there is Jacob the Cheater/Supplanter who, through no choice nor deeds of his own -- only that God had said, *"Jacob have I loved, Esau I have hated"*[177] -- had his name changed to Israel -- "He who would be prince with God." All his sons who sold Joseph into slavery nevertheless founded tribal dynasties, which are promised restoration at the Last Day. And even though Jacob's name was changed by God to Israel, still from then on out the two names, "Jacob/Cheater" and "Israel/Prince-with-God," are used interchangeably in scripture, both to describe God's people and also their founder. He is the God of Jacob – "Supplanter/Cheater" -- as much as He is the God of Israel – "He who would be prince with God."

Somebody's playing a real big trick on us here. We have really thick skulls or we would get it.

But like I said, I don't know what went through Pharaoh's mind. I can't begin to figure out for him what level of responsibility he had for his "own" choices. Paul pretty much stops that argument anyway when he says, *"How can the pot say to the potter, how could you have made me this way?"*[178]

He says in other places some vessels are appointed for honor and some for dishonor, some for glory and some for destruction. Before Jacob or Esau was born, He (GOD) said He hated one, and loved the other. You just can't argue with it. It just is.

Ok, now here's where I start saying the opposite of what I've just written above, and tell you that it just depends on which wagon you hitch your team to. I mean, there's the grace wagon and there's the "I'll be my own god" wagon. And Paul says that, too. "Hey, gang, everything is God doing it, but oh by the way, you are responsible for your life and what you choose and which way you go."

Yikes!

The grace wagon doesn't know that other side of things. I'll say it again. I don't understand Pharaoh's deal. I don't understand Judas' deal. I don't know why Jezebel became Jezebel and Ahab her husband was the most wicked king of Israel. But Jezebel and Ahab brought forth Elijah the Tishbite, and his spiritual son Elisha. You can say they followed the devil because they were his children but <u>why</u> did they follow the devil and not the Lord? I don't know.

What I'm trying to say is that I can't write a textbook answer to this responsibility dilemma, because I have no frame of reference for it. From the perspective of the Kingdom of God, the Kingdom of Grace, there is no responsibility question, because we find ourselves only in Him, He living as ourselves, without the least shade of separation. This not of ourselves, by anything we have thought or done or even believed or chosen by ourselves, but by mercy and grace as a gift, so that by grace we choose Him as we have been chosen in Him before the foundation of the earth, and we know no other will nor life except,

"My meat is to do the will of Him who sent me, and finish His work."[179]

How did we come by this? We do not know! *"Then shall two be in the field; the one shall be taken, and the other left."*[180] Can we explain that?

Years ago, when I was a young man, I had many friends, all of us coming up at the same time, experiencing the same things, hit with the same problems, the same obstacles. Somehow I got singled out of my bunch. Jesus came walking by my gas station where I worked and said, *"Follow me, and I'll make you a fisher of men."*

Maybe he said it to others and they weren't paying attention, I don't know. Why did I hear, and the "others" did not? I went and told them to the best of my ability but for most of them it went in one ear and out the other. Why? I don't know. I don't know why I read, *"A thousand shall fall at thy side, and ten thousand at thy right hand; but it shall not come nigh thee,"*[181] and I believe it, and others don't believe it. I don't know why that is.

Which brings me back to prayer. These days [at the time of this writing] God has me going three times a week to "cardio-rehab." So this morning I went in and according to the charts, it was time for my upgrade to the next level -- longer periods of exercise. So today I'm doing the treadmill, looking into the mirror in front of me, which enables me not only to see myself, but also everybody else in the room.

Out of the blue, prayer just fills me up, and I'm almost weeping (have to do it inwardly because they'd get concerned if they saw somebody weeping at cardio-rehab, unlike the Pentecostal church), because I'm praying about everything, naming everything before me going on in my life as Christ manifesting Himself. Then I found myself looking around the room, and one by one I saw each of them and saw them in Christ, and pronounced God's blessings on each one as the Spirit gave it to me in the moment. The "prayer life" I sought all those years ago, thinking somehow it was something to which I could attain by much fervor, is just spontaneously the Life of the Spirit in me every day. It was back then, too, but I hadn't recognized it yet.

I saw a man on Oprah this afternoon, just caught the last minute or so of his interview. He apparently had been talking about how alcohol abuse had destroyed his life, and how he had been very wealthy, worth some $20 million, and had lost everything because of his addiction and had been reduced to doing custodial work and cleaning other people's toilets just to get by.

Oprah asked him how could he bear that, and the man had really the most absolutely wonderful answer. He said, "I had to lose everything, Oprah, and I had to clean other people's toilets. I lived because of it."

Stripped of everything else but the Living God, you are nothing but prayer because every moment is God creating anew the universe and you are His son whom He eternally begets THIS day, and you are the light of your world and the salt of your earth.

And all those who appear as your enemies, whether outwardly or inwardly, your "negatives," your thorns in the flesh, your Egyptians, whatever term you give them, are to a man servants of the Lord and do His will. We do not live of the flesh, are not of the flesh, and do not see after the flesh. We see only Life, and only the building up of the Kingdom of God.

When you are His, (and all are His), everything He intends toward you is Life for you for others. Everything. No enemy can harm you, dissuade you, prevent you, or discourage you, because He has chosen you, and seen you in Him before the foundation of the earth, and no one can thwart His will.

This gives us a great freedom, and it is the only freedom that matters, because it is the freedom of needing no protection nor safety nets for ourselves, and the very fearful freedom of having no presumption of assured rescue, and without that presumption we are nonetheless free to go into hell itself as God leads to deliver the captives.

That's the only "side" to any question that I see. I don't see any other "side" except the Living God Who is All in all.

Make peace with thine adversary quickly -- and then you see clearly what comes next.

Ps 119:89-91

89 For ever, O LORD, thy word is settled in heaven.

90 Thy faithfullness is unto all generations: thou hast established the earth, and it abideth.

91 They continue this day according to thine ordinances: for all are thy servants.

Haven't We Left Sin Behind?

Someone recently asked me if I thought Abraham had sinned with Hagar. My first reply was, "Why are you asking sin questions?"

Though we preach and teach continuously that in Christ's death and resurrection we have no more to do with sin and sins, (*"God forbid,"* as Paul said, that we should *"sin that grace may abound"*[182]), and that now we live, tempted always with the possibility of sin, in the land of righteousness and grace only, still the question pops up over and over.

But haven't we left that behind? If a bit in one form or another here and there crops up, no big deal; we recognize, confess the truth, repent (change our mind), and go on.

I was thinking today about car repair. Last week I replaced the starter in my car. It had been giving me trouble for a while, making a real nuisance of itself. But eventually my sinning car was forcibly taken to the shop and had its starter replaced. That was last week. Today I was driving somewhere and I remembered all the inconvenience and hassle of having a bum starter last week, and then I realized how it was absolutely gone now from my consciousness since the car was behaving "as if it had never had a starter problem." Though I do remember last week and before when the inconveniences occurred, still they have disappeared from my current consciousness now that the problem is solved. I no longer have a "bad-starter consciousness."

Now our "problem" was sin and a continual consciousness of sin, and we know the origin of sin, which means that our former "sin problem" did not even originate in ourselves, though it is "in ourselves" that the solution has to be born.

Now the solution, as we know, is that in the cross, Sin, the Devil, has been cast out of us and we ourselves have now become the Holy of Holies in our innermost selves. In our center are the Mercy Seat and Aaron's Rod that Buds and the Bread from Heaven and the Holy Presence.

This is all that is in our center now, but in order for it to be "birthed" in our inner consciousness, so that heaven and earth come into alignment together in our inner awareness, we come progressively to realize that we are "beloved sons, in whom [God is] well pleased," and that sin does not enter God's mind, and what we are all progressively realizing and experiencing is the peace of God, Who finds no fault in us and has no condemnation toward us.[183]

Instead of continual disapproval and constant correction because we never measure up, in this new kingdom, God is in us as continual comfort, joy, peace, thanksgiving, praise, wonder, awe, life, blessing, abundance, truth, reality, and love. God is not in the business of condemning us, punishing us, thinking ill of us, but only of uplifting and blessing us and being in us the outgoing power to heal the nations (other folks) in and as the odd you and me. If there is any correction and upbraiding from the Father, it is in order that we might come to the end of what we think is our separate selves, our supposed "own" righteousness, strength and holiness.

We must first learn to the uttermost that we are nothing in ourselves and God is All in all, and that He finds us <u>pleasing to Him</u> because He has made us to be expressions of Himself. He has said that <u>in our day,</u> *"I will dwell in them and walk in them and be their God."*[184]

Here we are speaking of something much more than some separate anthropomorphic "Being" way off in the sky to whom we all owe allegiance, as if he is some sort of political king. Instead He IS every breath we breathe, every vision we see, every thought we think, and every motivation of our true inner heart. *"In Him we live and move and have our being."*[185]

When we once catch that and realize we didn't make ourselves, had absolutely nothing to do with "making ourselves," -- *"It is He who hath made us, and not we ourselves"*[186] -- that He is completely the potter and we completely the clay, in that undoing we have lost our "own" life. And in that "death" we retain no sort of ability to choose, to will, to think, to know the difference between truth and lie, since we have nothing to bring to the table, nothing to offer to get the prize. Even our own life if we could give it would not even approach the value of the Gift, but then we find that it is ours "without money and without price," and from then on we have nothing more to do with sin or with sin questions. It (sin) is not a matter anymore between the Lord and us, and can be as forgotten as my last week's faulty starter. The starter is fixed now, the car starts -- who wants to think about how it was last week or to anticipate every moment of the day how my starter might go out again?

I just don't worry about sin! Fahgeddaboudit!!!! God has said to anyone who will hear, *"Thou art my beloved son, in whom I am well pleased."* When you hear that word within you, you arise from the water of baptism, maybe take a side-route into the desert for awhile, but come back in the power of the Spirit to *"go about doing good and healing all who are oppressed of the devil, for God is with [you.]"*[187] You haven't got time nor an inclination to sin, because you are too busy doing the Father's will.

This is where we find we "always do his will." How can that be, since it does not seem like that? Because we have learned to see the invisible and to know that is the real, and to trust God in what is Real, and to leave all to him, reserving nothing at all to do, to be, to think, to say, for ourselves. And then you find that you actually, truly do His will, you work His works, you think His thoughts, you speak His words. Not by <u>one thing whatsoever</u> you do humanly, but because He lives in you and does the works, all of them, from A-Z, alpha to omega, start to bottom, totally. (What would anyone reserve for himself?)

And even if we do slip and sin, it works something positive. Everything, good or evil, right or wrong, gentle and loving or hateful and violent, works the work of God to the good of those who love Him and are the called according to His purpose.

"In the world ye shall have tribulation, but be of good cheer, I have overcome the world."[188] Now, that might not seem to be such good news, if Jesus has *"overcome the world,"* but He still lives way off up in heaven in some blissful beatific state. It IS good news if He has come to live in us and take over the dying in us to make it His dying, and to take over the living in us by being the life that is manifested out of our mortal flesh. When Jesus was way off up in heaven in my consciousness, it didn't seem to help me that much if Jesus had overcome the world, but if in the midst of my "tribulations," He has overcome the world in ME, which I

now know to be the Truth, then that is good news, great news, the best news indeed!

No more sin. The sacrifice once offered has taken away a consciousness of sins once for all. We no longer live in it. It's gone. As far as the east is from the west. (Heb 10, Rom 6, etc.)[189]There is simply nothing more to say, except to encourage us all to rise up, to drop the graveclothes of shame, condemnation, self-disparagement (all of which are out of the "pride of self"), and to affirm the truth, "God is mighty in ME!" and "rivers of living water" are flowing out of our bellies![190]

Just say it.

Loving the Sinner Hating the Sin

The term, "love the sinner but hate the sin" has never set well with me. I know the intent, but somehow I've never made peace with the expression. It seems to me a "separated" expression. God loved us unequivocally when we were unlovable to ourselves and others, when we were full of pride, greed and lust, and that same Love He loved us with then (when we were his "enemies") is the same Love-for-others that comes out of us now. Where would "hate" be involved?

Jesus for the most part didn't come preaching against specific sins of men, except for the pride and judgment of the "scribes, Pharisees, hypocrites." In fact, often people would come up to Jesus and try to get Him to condemn certain people or acts, trying to "tempt him in his speech," so that they could prove he was not the Son of God because He associated with "sinful" people. In their minds, if they could get him to condemn His "sinner" friends, he would seem a hypocrite for hanging out with them and for not rebuking them all day long for their many sins and immoralities. Or, if that didn't work, they were looking for Him to betray his supposed disrespect for the Law by somehow getting him to condone sin and transgressions of the law. If they couldn't prove Him untrue by the inconsistencies of his so-called "compassion," He could surely be proved an enemy of God because He would not uphold God's laws.

But Jesus would not be drawn into their game.

So then a mob of angry self-righteous men dragged a possibly half-naked provocative woman, (who perhaps threatened all of them with her sensuality because they probably all wanted her), who had been caught in the act, the very act, of adultery. That means they broke in on her when she and her lover were "doing it," and were probably watching her beforehand. Not a very noble enterprise for "righteous" men. Then they pulled that woman out of bed, pulling her out of coitus itself maybe, with violence, malice and rancor, probably shielding their eyes so they wouldn't be tainted and stirred by the sight of her wet sex and thus incite their own lust. Then they dragged her no doubt kicking and screaming to the Master for his pronouncement of judgment.

They threw her down in front of Him and said, "Master, here we have a woman caught in the act, the very act, of adultery! What about THAT? What are you going to do about THAT? She was committing adultery! Do you hear? The law says we have to stone her, but what do You say?" (They were right according to the law. Such a one, according to the law of Moses, was worthy of death by stoning.)

But Jesus seemed unconcerned about the "sin." Certainly he understood what transgression had taken place. But there was no acknowledgement of that, no convening a tribunal to see whether what these men said was true. Not a shadow of condemnation for her. No hint of disapproval, no disappointment, no projection of "shame on you," only a simple sentence to all those standing around in seething hatred with rocks in their hands, standing at the ready to brutalize and murder this transgressor: *"Let him who is without sin among you cast the first stone."*[191]

It is not insignificant that there was One standing among them, the same One Who spoke, in whom there was no sin, and He did not pick up a stone. The only one who could righteously pronounce "judgment" and administer the scripture-required punishment, stoning to death, was Jesus, and He showed no interest in doing so. As the men left one by one, so that finally there was no one left except she and the Lamb, He asked, *"Where are your accusers?"* She replied, *"No one has condemned me, Lord."* Then He said, *"Neither do I condemn thee, go thou and sin no more."*

He had no judgment, no condemnation for her. To the normal everyday hurting people who came to him -- outcasts, maimed, sick, infirm, possessed of devils, unsuccessful, prodigal -- He spoke of glory, compassion and forgiveness, and saw them as sheep who only needed the right shepherd.

Even though Biblical language sometimes puts the world into two camps, the terms "sinners" and "saints" have become distasteful to me in current usage. For one thing, though some might claim to know, I have a tremendous difficulty telling the difference. It's not so black and white to me as I thought it was in my spiritual infancy. Back then I thought I was in intimate fellowship with anyone who had prayed "the sinner's prayer." And likewise I had no fellowship with someone who had not. But many years' experience has taught me that it isn't always automatic that those who say they are my brothers are truly my brothers in their own hearts. Likewise, those who often have appeared to me to belong to the "other" camp, I have sometimes found as in tune with righteousness, truth, and love, as the most truly "Christian" I have known.

God "separated Paul from his mother's womb," and brought Him to the "road to Damascus," and then on through His career as God's "chosen vessel" to testify to the Gentiles. You see God's hand in Paul from birth on, not just starting with the Damascus road experience. Therefore, even though Saul became the enemy of the church, God, whose ways are higher than our ways, whose thoughts are higher than our thoughts, was molding Paul by those very experiences, and Paul was uniquely PAUL by having been the persecutor of the saints and a "Pharisee of Pharisees."

You get the idea from the Gospels that the "sinners" didn't hang around the "holy people" too much. The stink of disapproval must've been so strong when they were around that the "holy people" they were too condemned to even be around them.

The supposed "holy" people no doubt blamed any guilt and condemnation the "sinners" felt on the poor "sinners" themselves, who after all, were only sleeping in the beds they had made for themselves. And they certainly didn't want to be "tainted" with contact with them. From the perspective of the self-righteously holy, it is the "sinners" who put up any barriers by their deeds.

But Divine Love loves unequivocally without discrimination and it is pure, seeing all that it loves as pure. It is the burden and job of the Sons of God to remove the barriers, to level walls with love. To not even see sin if necessary.

When it says in 1 Cor 13 that, *"love rejoiceth not at iniquity,"* Paul is not meaning "taking a stand against sin," in the traditional sense, such as standing against a whole bunch of fleshly deeds – "We don't smoke, we don't chew, and we don't go with girls that do."

But real iniquity is found primarily in judgment that comes out of pride. Love lifts up. If a woman beset with sins came into a room where Jesus was sitting, Jesus would say, "*Woman, thy sins are forgiven thee.*" People in the room might get angry, because they might think that "wicked one" hasn't yet dealt her "sins," and they may all know it. But He said to the thief on the Cross, who had never dealt with his "sins," "*This Day shalt thou be with me in Paradise.*"[192]

How much more does He say that all day long to all His lost sheep in all their "sins" in all times in all places in the earth?

If we would see the Truth then we would see Only Christ in all. But how can we see Christ if He is not there in another person's faith? Because it is OUR job to see the truth as we have been given it, and that vision is what we impart.[193] Imparting God's vision in a person before he sees it for himself – isn't this what the prophets did? God only sees Himself in each, whether sinner or saint, and all have the opportunity for the same vision, which is, "*as many as received Him had power to become the sons of God.*"[194] And in those who receive Him, God's vision of Himself in His Sons is complete and All in all.

Searching For God

Is "doubt" the opposite of faith, or is "unbelief?" Is "doubt" sin? Now that might seem nitpicky about a word but the meanings of the words are very different to me. Doubt is a state of mind in which "I'm not sure, I don't know, I can't tell," are the predominant themes, and we don't know yet which way the doubt will go. "Unbelief" is active will, resisting the wind of the Spirit by being wrapped in its own self-image, for a time.

Jesus performed the most incredible miracles the world has ever seen. He was transfigured with heavenly light and talked with Moses and Elijah on top of a mountain. Jesus prevailed over Satan in his trial in the desert after going without food for forty days. He raised the dead, restored sight, cleansed lepers, and fed thousands of people more than once with next to nothing. He gave the greatest sermon of all time as related in John 14-17. Yet after all that, the Son of God went through severe "doubt" in Gethsemane, even though He had repeatedly said the Cross was the purpose for which He was born. After having testified publicly that, *I and my Father are One*," and, "*The works that I do, the Father does them*," he still questioned himself as if He was a "separate self," who maybe had been wrong all along about the will of the Father. Maybe God's will was something else -- wasn't that what He was asking when He wondered if there could be another way?

Still Jesus, in the midst of His doubts and questionings, was rescued and propelled into faith by the Spirit, so that He walked through to the end in the blinders of faith and was filled by a strength that upheld Him in His final weakness.

In questioning these things as I pondered them I had my own mini Gethsemane, wondering for a moment had I been saying the wrong things, had I gone out too far on a limb, and in the midst of that suddenly "I AM" popped into my head.

Here is the mystery of God....

When you were a kid did you ever look up at the night sky and try to imagine infinity? It breaks your mind.

God, in plain common language, at least since the time of Moses, has been telling us His name.

"I AM."

I read a book years ago, some esoteric mystery, and the hero gets to the apartment where an important computer is, because of course he needs the files on that computer to save the world or his behind, I forget which, (same difference to him I guess). He turns on the computer and when the screen comes up it reads, "DO YOU KNOW THE PASSWORD?"

So he starts typing passwords, anything he can think of, especially things he knew about the person – birthday, kids names, etc. He tries for hours and nothing works. The screen continues to say nothing except, "DO YOU KNOW THE PASSWORD?" and his time is running out. Finally out of sheer desperation he types, "N-O", into the computer.

And the pot of gold was his....

The answer was TOO obvious, so it was overlooked.

<u>"*I AM*" is in first person.</u>

God didn't tell Moses to announce to the Egyptians, "HE IS sent me." He told Moses to say, "*I AM sent me.*"

Moses was to say God's name the only way it can be said, in the first person -- "*I AM.*"

And likewise, when we say God's name, we can only say it in the first person -- "*I AM.*"

Tricky of God, isn't it?

Why is it then that we can only say His Name in first person? Because HE is the Only One who ever uttered "I AM." We say, "i am" as an echo of the same one I AM, but there is only one I AM. And we are OF the only One I AM.

We may describe it to be something like standing at the edge of a precipice in a rocky gorge, and yelling out at the top of your lungs, "I AM!," and then hearing the echo of your one spoken "I AM!" reverberating back and forth off the rock walls down the length of the gorge: i am i am i am i am i am. God is the one who yelled out into an empty universe that perhaps, like the scientists say, was at one point an infinitely dense singularity (which by the way I can no more conceive of than I can infinity). And when He yelled out, "I AM!," things started popping! "Lights, Camera, Action!" Deity is unfolding eternally nothing but Himself, nothing but "I AM," and everything echoes and restates that which He has Eternally Said. What will be contrary has the freedom to do so, but we are not talking of that.

Now, the implication of this first person business is this: the "I" who utters, "I AM," and the "i" who returns the echo "i am," are the same "I". At the foundation of all things one cannot separate one from the other. There is only one true "I". All other "I's" are out of, or derivatives of, the only one true "I."

And that obvious, in our face, NAME, "*I AM,*" has been there all along. While we've been sifting around, looking for other passwords.

Reminds me of what someone said: "Searching for God is kind of like looking for your glasses when you have them on."

In other words, quit looking up toward heaven for another god to come down and rescue you, save you, help you. No one is up there.

Look in yourself. There is a He, and there is a you, but joined together as one.[195] *I AM* is first person. Who are You talking about when you say, "*I AM*"?

...One more point to make is that inherent in the word "unbelief" is something more than passive to me, implying "action" has gone into making "unbelief" to become something more than doubt. It has taken the "right negative" -- doubt -- and made a "wrong positive" out of it. Faith must have "doubt" to swallow up as its engine to propel it.

"Unbelief" is simply faith in reverse, or "doubt" becoming the illusory reality of "unbelief" by our agreement with it. We are assaulted by "doubt" every moment of the day and countless times every day "*I AM*" rises up and dispels the doubt with the inner Word that then propels us into a new seeing of God in the present moment. This is our normal life in Christ. Unbelief is no longer our normal bailiwick, and we don't visit there too often anymore, because this wonderful inner settling has occurred in our inner being, where we've seen the Rock, we know the secret place of the Most High, and like Moses we've seen the Promised Land.

But unlike Moses in the flesh, who represented the Law, we do enter into the Promised Land and find rest, because TODAY we have heard His Voice, TODAY we have believed, TODAY "*we who have believed do enter into rest,*"[196] therefore TODAY we don't follow an "evil heart" into unbelief, because TODAY we have ceased from our own works, as God did from His.

TODAY the Word is:

Isaiah 30:

19 For the people shall dwell in Zion at Jerusalem: thou shalt weep no more: he will be very gracious unto thee at the voice of thy cry; when he shall hear it, he will answer thee.20 And though the Lord give you the bread of adversity, and the water of affliction, yet shall not thy teachers be removed into a corner any more, but thine eyes shall see thy teachers:21 And thine ears shall hear a word behind thee, saying, This is the way, walk ye in it, when ye turn to the right hand, and when ye turn to the left.29 Ye shall have a song, as in the night when a holy solemnity is kept; and gladness of heart, as when one goeth with a pipe to come into the mountain of the LORD, to the mighty One of Israel.

TODAY....

If You've Seen Me Then You've Seen The Father

"Blessed are the pure in heart, for they shall see God."[197]
It is the simplest thing, and it is under our nose, so close we can't see it. That is why this is so difficult to write about and even to wrap our minds around, because it is so simple.

Jesus said, "If you've seen Me, then you've seen the Father." ME? Who is "ME"?

Everything has only one purpose -- to effect the Incarnation throughout the whole of the universe. To manifest into the consciousness of every creature in heaven and earth that God IS ALL and in all, and from that an eternal outflow and expansion of love eternally in Christ.

The Incarnation is about God walking fully as Man. This is the only possible meaning of the Cross, so that God and man, God and creation, could be restored back into their original unity through Christ. The Fullness of the Godhead bodily.

Which brings us to the now. Now is the time. *"Blessed are the pure in heart, for they shall see God."* This is a more present reality than our brains can comprehend. We keep wanting to analyze it and tell how it works and why, or else make excuses for why it isn't quite so right now – "it's only positional after all" -- when it can never be grasped that way, since it IS. It can only be "known." And "known," means to BE it.

It is the Pearl of Great Price for which you sell all to buy. If the onion peels could be peeled off all at once (which would be too great a shock to our system and why Moses could only see God's "backside"), then we would see that right now, right here, the Kingdom of Heaven exists in all its fullness. Everywhere God is, Heaven is, and God is everywhere; therefore Heaven is everywhere. He is in no physical locality that you can identify, and yet He fills them all.

I've written these words maybe thousands of times now and they almost seem trite but they are so woefully inadequate to represent the truth they try to portray. This is no dogmatic point I seek to drive home. Just the testimony of the sweetness of Being, the Wholeness of God which any time, anywhere, and often at the oddest and most surprising moments, can break through and flow completely over us and draw our hearts and minds into the most subtle and sublime worship of the invisible Holy God. He is forever our intimate Friend Who is totally beyond ourselves, yet in the midst of and mixed with us, so that we living are He living. It is too great for us, and yet all that we are is He. Travel as far within or without that we want, we cannot get outside Him.

Now right here we are undone, yet raised to heights of glory we can only see in dimness, and can hardly utter until the day of their fulfillment in total clarity.

He is Lord of heaven AND earth. Heaven AND earth are full of His glory.[198] The prophet uses present tense. Right now, TODAY, the earth is full of His glory. Do you see it?

If we seek ourselves outside Christ then we seek a will'o the wisp, a non-existence for there is only one place where our life is found. *"Your life is hid in Christ in God"*[199] ... *When he shall appear, then shall you also appear in glory."*[200] Another way of putting *"I live yet not I but Christ liveth in me and the life I now live in the flesh."*[201]

We do know, don't we, that Galatians 2:20 is not a scientific formula, in which we have to determine what are the proper proportions of each part needed to get the equation to come out right? In this living reality, it only "works" when we come by grace to lose all and find ourselves undone into nothingness and then He rises up in us as the All of Who we are. From that death (*"I am crucified with Christ"*), we rise again not ourselves and yet more ourselves (*"I live yet not I, but Christ liveth"*) than we can comprehend, since we still see a city afar off, to which by grace we are drawn more fervently every moment. And as we trek along, the wake we create brings whiffs of glory to passersby who often turn, even unbeknownst to us, and walk in the sweet savor of life that follows us secretly wherever we go.

In hiddenness He shines forth from you -- you, the one whose "identity" He created that He might wear it as Himself -- as you are! He's a tiny babe in a manger, known only to a few maybe, but He grows into the full stature of Himself in us.

It does not depend on your "right-thinking," or on your "moment-by-moment believing," but on Him. *"He who keeps Israel neither slumbers nor sleeps."*[202] And He is faithful to be the expression of Himself He has determined from eternity to be in and AS you!

If it depended on "my [human] thinking" then I'd be bouncing around in and out of God and His kingdom millions of times a day as every possible thought runs through my head, some of them catching my attention for quite a while. If it depended on my "moment by moment believing" then it wouldn't be a free gift of grace. It wouldn't be love. God really wouldn't be my friend. He would be my boss and I'd be working off a debt, which I could never come close to repaying.

I spoke wedding vows only once. I've been married ever since, no matter how I've felt about it, whether I doubted it or believed in it. By our word we became married. And it has remained so from the moment of that confession.

It is the same in Christ. We have received Him, haven't we? The marriage ceremony has occurred. Now we're just working things out, and the final maturity of any marriage is that the two become one not only in idea and concept but in deed and unity of purpose and action, regardless of whatever different activities or varying interests the two may have. My wife and I do different things, yet we are one in every way.

But I get away from my main point, which is that we have "taken" or "received" Him within us, and He is the Whole ball of wax, and in HIM are all the promises of God fulfilled as a YES and an AMEN – It is finished! In Him all things consist and we are of Him and partake of His fullness, which flows out of us through no effort of our own.

We simply live in the recognition that He is living His own Divine Life in and through and as the person that is ourselves, and by His own will He is experiencing death in us and by that death manifesting life in our mortal flesh.

But still the one idea that we have the hardest time shaking is that there has just got to be <u>something</u> I have to do! NO, for ye <u>*are dead*</u>, and your life is <u>*hid with Christ in God*</u>! You don't depend on a dead person for anything. You look to the living! And the living person is invisibly, imperceptibly, YOU!!! (Christ having risen as you!)

"Show us the Father" -- "If you've seen ME, then you've seen the Father!" Where is HE??? You cannot look back into yourself to see yourself, and that is where God is, and there will never be any more of Him than there is in this present moment. And He will never be any more you and me than He is in this present moment. (We will only know it more.)

You just believe! (Which starts usually in some conscious "word" which we speak, and then as the reality of that Word is continually spoken back in us by the Spirit within, it then simply becomes a natural flow, which comes in fresh recognitions every day.)

Paul says we were chosen in Him before the foundation of the earth; therefore we are waking up to an eternal reality. This is not to bog us down in theological difficulties right here, but to see the unbelievably astounding thing -- i.e. that time and eternity are one, and we have the privilege of walking out in a moment by moment sequential life the expression of God's limitless eternal freedom in our lives.

Paul says, *"It pleased God, who separated me from my mother's womb, and called me by his grace, To reveal his Son in me, that I might preach Him among the heathen..."*[203] In other words, there is never a moment in life when His fullness is not at work accomplishing His will, and the "times" of our "awakenings" are determined by Him, and He is faithful to do it because He cannot deny Himself.

Therefore do not wait for the day of completion to believe that you are He living right now. Be Christ now! "Coming home" is seeing God fully in the present moment -- by faith. What you take takes you. *"Behold, I stand at the door, and knock: if any man hear my voice, and open the door, I will come in to him, and will sup with him, and he with me.*"[204] That's one of the first verses I heard and learned years ago. They told me it was true back then, and the years have more than confirmed their word.

Anything is possible from that moment on. Even the reconciliation of all things, or the salvation of the world.

Doctrines

Teaching and doctrines are important, and it is a good thing for us to spend some time working these things out and learning them, but from there the goal, as I see it, unless you've been called to be a "teacher," is to forget them and just live your life.

Who lives by a doctrine? You just live. I always use the example of marriage. I may go to a thousand marriage seminars, read a thousand books on how to have a good marriage, but in the end it's just my wife and I being together in spontaneity. The oneness of marriage between the two of us just IS, and can't be whumped up by memorizing and practicing the precepts taught in the "One Hundred Two Scriptural Principles To Obey To Have A Great Marriage" course. Marriage can't be formula because it is living life; and union with God can't be formula because He is Life.

The world really is all jumbled up. There are no classic cases, no book-perfect scenarios. It's all in the wind. There's a tension in everything, good and evil mixed up, hot and cold, predestination and free will, heaven and earth. Sometimes one seems to predominate in a given situation over the other, hot rules cold, or the next day cold rules hot, but the tension never goes away. You see saints in sinners and sinners in saints.

Obey the law and stone the adulterous woman (because that is the law under Moses, perfectly right and legal) or release her from the penalty of her sin in compassion (and apparent disregard for sin)?

Which is right?

Jesus, quoting from Hosea 6:6, said, "*But go ye and learn what that meaneth, I will have mercy, and not sacrifice.*"

As I see it, the only way through the jumble and the tension between what are always two reasonable sides is seeing God in love and compassion in every subatomic particle. There is no ill will. Anywhere. That which appears as "ill will" is masking in its freedom the greater Will. And that greater Will intends only life and freedom in love for all.

All creatures are created out of God's infinite freedom and He seems to have ordained that our journey should be out of the freedom from which we were formed into the bondage, and yet enlightenment, of self-consciousness, caught in the God-purposed trap of the wicked one, in order to be finally sprung into the glorious liberty of the sons of God.

Liberty -- freedom! The cry of mankind since it found its voice. Every creature seeks its freedom. And Freedom means simply being one with what you desire, do and are.

Can we define Jesus Christ – make a set of behavioral principles based on His example? No, I don't think so. I have tried.

He said He lived by the Spirit, which some people would take as being flighty. Daffy. One moment He's hanging out with a bunch of Pharisees; the next day He's been invited to a banquet with *"publicans and sinners."* But Jesus wasn't daffy. He knew very well what He was doing. He was walking in the fullness of His Father. But in the fullness of being human at the same time – as One. Responding to the needs of the moment in the relaxation of His own desires and actions being those of the Father, trusting the fullness of the Spirit to manifest out of His human life.

It was being bold about the source of His life that got Him in so much trouble with the establishment.

But that is the goal of our doctrinal study, that we might eventually drop it from the foreground of our minds, at least for ourselves (there are always those coming along that need these things), and just live our lives in the freedom and complete trust in the Lord that He is our manifested self in the world. We can obey Augustine's injunction to "love God and do what you like."

Sounds like license to some, liberty to others. Stench of death or aroma of life.

But here *"unto the pure thou wilt shew thyself pure"* comes into play. That verse, and its reverse side -- *"unto the froward thou wilt shew thyself froward"*[205] are out of a deep well.

But in a nutshell let me just say this. And it goes very much with what I said above. We live in one or another kingdom. Questions of choice, responsibility, permanence and duration are never solved on the human level. Because those answers are not merely intellectual, and are in the mystery of God.

But apart from those lofty ideas, *"unto the pure thou wilt shew thyself pure,"* simply means to me that when you begin to see All is God manifesting Himself on some level, you see at the whole foundation of everything the Love of God, and seeing that, you increasingly begin to see that everything that comes to you, or from you, is one or another form of the love of God, even if in flesh or devil disguise, and you begin from there to see that there is nothing that is outside His purview, thus making everything Holy, everything pure, since He is the basis of All, and manifests

Himself and only His own love purposes in everything there is, ever was, and ever shall be.

It changes everything to see that He is All in all.

It doesn't mean that you become an idiot or blind and can't see evil when it rises up. It doesn't mean you may not yourself in a position to defy or thwart evil in some way, for you may very well be called to such. But it does mean that first you see through that evil to the God Who purposed it for ultimate good, *"to save much people alive."*[206] And from there the path and purpose are clearer.

It also means that you can walk in freedom because no enemies can hurt you (since there really are no enemies). Having no enemies, not even death, means you have nothing to be protective over, and therefore are a clear lantern. A light with no impediment.

How do you get that? Become that "clear lantern?"

The answer is not hard to that question, is it? He Himself is the Clear Lantern, and guarantees His Own manifestation in our mortal flesh, without regard to our fleshly ability or commitment.

Doctrine then serves its purpose, much like the law, to take us to faith, but it is finally to faith it must take us, which means doctrine pushes us beyond itself into God Who Himself is our Living Doctrine.

"And this is the work of God, that ye believe on Him who He hath sent."[207]

That is it. Believe on Him. In You. As YOU! You're still you and always will be. But He's the "you" inside "you" as the "real you."

A Meditation on Psalm 10

10:1 Why standest thou afar off, O LORD? why hidest thou thyself in times of trouble?2 The wicked in his pride doth persecute the poor: let them be taken in the devices that they have imagined.3 For the wicked boasteth of his heart's desire, and blesseth the covetous, whom the LORD abhorreth.4 The wicked, through the pride of his countenance, will not seek after God: God is not in all his thoughts.5 His ways are always grievous; thy judgments are far above out of his sight: as for all his enemies, he puffeth at them.6 He hath said in his heart, I shall not be moved: for I shall never be in adversity.7 His mouth is full of cursing and deceit and fraud: under his tongue is mischief and vanity.8 He sitteth in the lurking places of the villages: in the secret places doth he murder the innocent: his eyes are privily set against the poor.9 He lieth in wait secretly as a lion in his den: he lieth in wait to catch the poor: he doth catch the poor, when he draweth him into his net.10 He croucheth, and humbleth himself, that the poor may fall by his strong ones.11 He hath said in his heart, God hath forgotten: he hideth his face; he will never see it.12 Arise, O LORD; O God, lift up thine hand: forget not the humble.13 Wherefore doth the wicked contemn God? he hath said in his heart, Thou wilt not require it.14 Thou hast seen it: for thou beholdest mischief and spite, to requite it with thy hand: the poor committeth himself unto thee; thou art the helper of the fatherless.15 Break thou the arm of the wicked and the evil man: seek out his wickedness till thou find none.16 The LORD is King for ever and ever: the heathen are perished out of his land.17 LORD, thou hast heard the desire of the humble: thou wilt prepare their heart, thou wilt cause thine ear to hear:

Let's imagine this scenario presented by David is not about all those wicked people over there, all those poor people over there, and the Lord God way up there. But rather see it, for a moment, as all taking place within us....

1 *"Why standest thou afar off, O LORD? why hidest thou thyself in times of trouble?"*

Isn't this the truth of things in the crucible? God is nowhere to be found. "There is no help for him in God," say the voices of the accusers. "He's a sinner!" shouts the crowd as they wheel you by in the wagon headed for the execution. "I must be," the thought occurs, as you see the vehemence of the crowd, their certain knowledge of your condition, their proud, "Ah-hah," that you who spoke the high things of God have been brought low. God, who only yesterday had seemed so real in His invisible Presence and brimming with promises, now almost seems a mockery of Himself, disappearing into the background and leaving a ravaging horde of accusers and maligners in charge.

"Surely I deserve this wrath," another thought comes. "They must be right. They are so many, and their case is strong. God has deserted me. Maybe I've never known Him at all, like they say. Who am I kidding?"

4 *"The wicked, through the pride of his countenance, will not seek after God: God is not in all his thoughts."*

Riding in the wagon, hands bound awaiting the axe, becoming almost oblivious to the taunts of the crowd, the Spirit breaks through. "Wait a minute," the sudden Light says, "God IS in all my thoughts." All those accusing voices, all their taunts, are only the taunts of voices seeking ascendancy over God, which can never be, for they have no life of their own. They are the devil's echo, because in their false life of self-ascendancy, in their continuous vain attempt to usurp life within me, they disbelieve in themselves as forms of God, and deny Him by not admitting that He is in all their thoughts.

The truth begins to burst in, though, knowing God IS in all our thoughts. Once caught, no escape. It is a wondrous liberating bondage of love. Though my wife and I may give little conscious thought to each other at times while doing the business of a normal day, still our presence is firm in each other in the subterranean foundation where we live, and neither of us do anything without full consideration of the other even though we are unconscious of it.

And in our heavenly love, with whom we've been bonded and made One Spirit in Christ Jesus, it is the same. We do our business, live our lives, slop the hogs, feed the chickens, and consciously or unconsciously, God is truly in all our thoughts.

A thousand moments a day open out into the Eternal. It may be only touches of a light breeze that we feel for just a moment, a look in an eye, or a train going by. Love is rampant in everything.

In 1985 I blessed and thanked God that he had "delivered me" from the yarn mill I had worked in for nearly five years on the all-night shift, and had put me into a full-time ministry. During those years at the mill, working through the night, the Spirit taught me every night. I could read without glasses then, even small print, and I had a little New Testament I kept in my back pocket and I read it every chance I got while on shift. Nobody minded, as long as you were discreet.

Sometimes I would go to the back door and open it and look outside into the night. We were in a rural area and there were woods across the parking lot, so even though I was in a factory with the unnatural, metallic sounds of machinery so loud you had to shout to be heard and earplugs were a OSHA-required necessity, I still could look out that back door in the middle of the night. Closing the thick door behind me, the machine sounds completely dissipated and almost instantly I would hear thousands of buzzing insects and all the other forest sounds in the deep middle of the night. On clear nights I basked under the stars, while they twinkled their praises through the thick summer air. In winter they were crisp and undiffused in their light, praising Him in their steady unbroken stream of revelation onto the face of the whole earth.

Then I would walk back inside, opening the door to a sudden, deafening cacophony of hundreds of machines sorting, spinning, clanging, starting and stopping; people going by to and fro, pushing carts, carrying clipboards, doffers doffing, spinners spinning and fixers fixing. And somehow the two (outside and inside) were together.

While I was so glad to get "delivered" from there, I look back on it now and marvel at how much and how wonderfully the Spirit spoke to me those years I worked there. Love is rampant. It is every moment of every day, whether we see it or not. God IS in all our thoughts. "I will never leave you nor forsake you."

8 "He [the wicked] sitteth in the lurking places of the villages: in the secret places doth he murder the innocent: his eyes are privily set against the poor."

Again those voices of the rabble pipe up, rebelling once again in futility, pointing out our poverty. And they are right to accuse us of being poor, because we truly have nothing. Our poverty, they assert, is our own fault, because we are not the innocent, and we have blood on our hands.

They lay a legal claim to our death, that it is not murder, and that we deserve our fate. And there is a legitimacy to their claim, which is why it is impossible to honestly dismiss it.

But now that we are led again like lambs to the slaughter, the foolish voices have no realization of what they've done. They intended murder and oppression, but didn't know that we had sold all we had to buy the field which contained the Pearl of Great Price, that our poverty is freely received, and we lie buried at the foot of a cross. They didn't know that to lose your life is to find it, and instead sought to save theirs only to lose them.

In our tears day and night we sought only to lose our lives, to *"bind the sacrifice with cords, even unto the horns of the altar,"* until that great Day when the Lord appeared in our midst and declared us dead to the world and alive unto Him and He Himself as our very Self. Heretofore we had hated our lives, abhorred ourselves, and sought only to be delivered from that which we hated. Gladly we laid the unclean thing at the foot of the Cross, wanting only to be rid of it, to cast it off, to be naked, bare, dead to who we were. We were glad just to be rid of it, having no inkling of what would come further along.

To be "poor" is to have no life of our own, but only an empty place for God to fill. "Innocence" is the quality of childhood that springs out of the Eternal, where all is wonder and new and there is no law and no condemnation. Innocence is possible to the poor because in this poverty there is no sin or remembrance of sin. It is buried and left in the tomb with the empty shroud. We arise in "newness of life," another way of saying "innocence." Since every moment we live the Heavenly Love is pouring out of the

Invisible, by it we are inwardly inebriated by the perking distillery of the Spirit, continuously sippin'"white lightnin'" from on high. Life IS wonder! It IS joy. It IS holiness. It is pure, righteous and guileless in its innermost center, with the innocence of an unblemished Lamb in the heart of all.

12 Arise, O LORD; O God, lift up thine hand: forget not the humble.

15 Break thou the arm of the wicked and the evil man: seek out his wickedness till thou find none.

16 The LORD is King for ever and ever: the heathen are perished out of his land.17 LORD, thou hast heard the desire of the humble: thou wilt prepare their heart, thou wilt cause thine ear to hear:

Having never forgotten us for one moment, even though He seemed to have disappeared completely from the landscape, the Living God arises. He lifts up the hand of His deliverance. The voices in the crowd know of His arrival, and one by one, as He questions them as to their validity, they acknowledge their error and dissolve into dust. There is now only One Voice left, <u>for the wicked and heathen are perished from the land, the land that we are</u>, and exist no more. We are raised ourselves from that dust, from the swirling vortex of confusion, from our poverty and weakness, in the Power of His Spirit.

WE arise! The whole creation has groaned and churned for this day! THIS is the DAY the Lord hath made!

"The Lord is in His holy temple. Let all the earth keep silence before Him."

The "earth" is the dust that we are, and we live in our poverty eternally in the center of His cross. And, The

Lord is now in the Holy Temple that we are, and we are the mighty power of God.

The heathen has perished in our land. The Eternal High Priest ever liveth to make intercession for us, and there is no more remembrance of sin. He has searched out the wickedness of the wicked, until he found NONE (in us).

There are times when what we have taken in faith before, has now become to us the evidence of our naiveté or romanticism. We are our own accuser, defendant, judge, and would-be executioner.

"How long, O Lord?"[208] the Psalmist cries. *"O God, thou knowest my foolishness; and my sins are not hid from thee."*[209]

We imagine the worst. We've done this to ourselves. We stepped foolishly too far out onto the limb, and now our folly will be revealed. No person of God are we! No, we are beset with sorrow, discord, confusion, guilt, torment, the swirl of the opinions of men, the weight of the whole of life and all we've done and heard and known and hoped for and sorrowed over, beating down on us, and being a cargo beyond bearing.

I wish I could say that right then and there a big light appears out of nowhere and a truck pulls up and we win the lottery. But it doesn't happen that way. Not usually.

Welcome to the work of God.

As workers in this kingdom, you get to suffer privation, sorrow, heartache, pain, catastrophe, inconvenience, self-doubt, intellectual-doubt, emotional-doubt, is-there-a--God-doubt, as well as all the things everybody else in the world has to worry about.

There are perks in the present moment. In the present moment you know the Solid Rock. El Shaddai has spoken in the desert and you have heard Him and He has proven Himself over and over by signs and wonders. You know. He will never leave you or forsake you.

But now our joints are poured out like water. And no end seems to be in sight. And maybe we've gotten it all wrong.

When you pour salt into the soup, where does the salt go? It dissolves out of distinctiveness, and saltiness permeates the soup.

Salt does not promote itself, but instead gives savor to other things. It brings out the taste, the life. For the salt to do its job, it has to in a sense lose itself, its particular self, and become completely one with the rest of the soup.

Forgive me for sounding Kung-fu-ey here, but the analogy is true.

When the salt loses its particular-ness, it melds into the other ingredients in the soup, taking them into itself as they take the salt into themselves.

The world around us is churning with fear and trembling right now. Not one of us is for sure day-by-day what is the right thing to do, and there is worldwide fear and great uncertainty.

But God has not deserted us. He always leaves a remnant.

The remnant is the salt of the earth. It takes the earth into itself, as it looses its saltiness throughout all the earth.

Since we are the salt of the earth, we take the earth into ourselves, churning up and down with every wave of our own and the rest of humanity's fears and joys. It must needs be, even though we wish it were not so and we think there is something wrong with us because we experience and feel all this.

Despite all our theological training, which should lead to rational-spiritual thinking, most of us think there's something wrong with us if we're feeling or experiencing "negative" things.

And that's ok, because that's all part of the process. We MUST "feel like" we're wrong. Whether imaginary or real, doesn't matter. (Hard to tell the difference anyway.)

Here is where salt and light meet. For the joy of salt is to lose itself through spreading its saltiness into everything else, and the joy of light is to shine on and show something else. All we actually see is light, but light reflecting off a dark body, giving it definition, shape and color.

"You are the light of the world," means that you by your life give the world light – definition, shape and color. Having grown up into Him, existing in Him Who is our Head, our very presence is the universal-creating fiat of the Word of God.

Your life, as you are right now, is the living real expression of the Living God. Open your eyes and believe. It's okay to be afraid and to think it can't be so. Believe anyway.

In the pit of hell honesty comes. And the sum total of honesty is this: whatever we put on ourselves is vanity in some form. Vanity is swept away as a power in the coming of the Risen One Who we find to be rising in us.

I fight it every time. But there is no life without death.

It is continuous in the present moment, and unboundedly at the same time tinged with golden light unseen to mortal eyes. Every death is precious as the seed of life it generates.

"Bearing about in the body the dying of the Lord Jesus"[210] is part and parcel of living in this world. All humanity is a participant. How does the song go, "Heaven came

down and glory filled my soul." I think that's it. <u>Heaven comes down and glory fills everything</u>. That's called "the Incarnation."

I fear I appear morbid but I don't mean to be so. Because there's an upshot to all this. There is a lot of "death" and it seems continuous. Little or big, it's always something.

But somehow someway if you look at it just right, squint maybe a little bit and cock your head to the right or left (according to your politics), you'll just pick up a glimpse, fleeting maybe, of the all-encompassing El Shaddai, God Almighty, Father of All, Who is through all, in all, and IS all. That glimpse, deep only in our faith, hardly by sight, is the resurrection light.

The resurrection is the power of GOD, which doesn't necessarily have visible or tangible evidence. It is the inner word of God spoken in our spirits, which presses upon us as a more tangible reality than that which we can feel with our fingers or see with our eyes.

But that more tangible reality has a way of leaking out of us, by hook or by crook, because we live, yet not we, but He lives.

So be the salt of the earth, not afraid of its smells and odors and heat. It will eat you up, but you will permeate it.

And be the light of the world. You already are.

Spirit Is Person

We define spirit as self, both in God and in man. It is the whole basis of what we have seen and what we say.

We develop this scripturally by starting out with Jesus' word to the woman at the well: "*God is Spirit, and they who worship Him worship Him in Spirit and in truth.*"[211]

If, then, "God is Spirit," and since God gave His name as "I AM," therefore Spirit IS Self -- "I AM."

Then further, the scriptures say God is the, "*father of spirits,*"[212] and, "*The spirit of man is the candle of the LORD, searching all the inward parts of the belly.*"[213] Both these passages give us an "organic" tie to the Father. Rather than the "spirit of man" being created out of "nothing," the indication here is a bond like that of parent to child, where the child comes forth out of the essence of its parents. "Father of spirits" gives us the familial tie, whereas "candle of the Lord" give us an ontological tie, that is, that we are tied to or come forth from God in the innermost part of our being. We have our "BE-ING" in God. This leads us to see that inwardly in the depths of all humanity is the Life of God, that He is the "*light that lights every man that comes into the world.*"[214]

The creation story gives further weight to this, when it says God "*breathed into his nostrils the breath of life.*"[215] We know in Scripture over and over "breath" and "wind" are synonymous with His Spirit. So it was by God's Spirit breathed into man that man became a living being -- "I am."

So, in the innermost part of ourselves, we are spirit. We are "I am."

It remains then to understand what Spirit is and what it means to "know" Spirit.

We "define" spirit as desire or love, knowing, and will or choosing. And this is to be understood as the most inward type of love or desire, the most inward type of "knowing" or knowledge, and the most inward will or choosing. In other words, we are speaking of our true selves, deeper than the normal everyday consciousness we mostly experience, and the issues we deal with there.

Before I say more about the union between the human spirit and the Deity, let me brush on Spirit just a moment. Because I think we head into deep waters here.

This is how I understand spirit. All is Spirit. Spirit is the true reality. To speak of Spirit we use terminology that has to do with time and space, which is all we understand, but Spirit is not of time and space, though Spirit is manifest in time and space, and time and space ARE spirit. There is no distance in spirit; there is no time. There is no here and there is no there.

Now God IS Spirit, and God IS Person, therefore ALL that is manifest, is the out-flooding of the Living God as Person outpouring Himself to be inner living truth of everything that is. Everything has its "being" (existence) in the eternal Reality which is God All in all, Who is Spirit.

But this, in and of itself, is not our salvation. The entire universe is a "oneness," as even scientists are saying, but that knowledge does nothing for us.

For to find ourselves after we have been prodigals, which is true for us all, we have to come home to our Father. And in coming home to our Father, the Eternal Person, we find our own personhood, which is hidden with Christ in God.

Even though humanity swims in a sea of God, walks in and breathes the breath of God, and lives in an environment that purposely testifies to the glory of God and shows His handiwork in every part and parcel of it, still humanity is far from Him. Because as certain as it is that at the depth of our being lies the entrance to Heaven and to God, that way is barred. We don't have the wherewithal in ourselves to crash the gates and take heaven for ourselves, even if we could find the entryway.

It is also certain that there is an opposite portal deep in our being, in the depths of ourselves which is spirit, which opens up into an interior unlimitedness, and where there is also the kingdom of wrath and darkness, the kingdom of the devil, powered by self-love, of which in our natural life we were captives and blinded to the light of God. We knew no other way, and thus we lived his grasping, needy and looking-out for-ol'-number-one way, as the whole of our race does. We are "spirits in prison," held captive by him, deceived by him, BUT (and this is a BIG "but") not yet having gone down with him into his portal and become willingly his devil-partners.

Still, however, we all live lives based on self-for-self, me-for-me. Even the most altruistic and seemingly unselfish among us, at the basis of ourselves if we were honest, would admit to living for ourselves. *"All is vanity,"*[216] says the Preacher in Ecclesiastes. He's searched the world over, learned the wisdom of all things in this world, seen everything there was to see, experienced everything there was to experience and concluded, "all is vanity." Why? Because caught in the blindness of his spirit, the wool pulled over his eyes in his innermost being, he could not break through the layer of separation and disharmony;

he could not break through the almost infinite pall of selfishness that seemed to pervade and color everything in his existence. So what if he had a thousand wives? So what if he had more gold than a hundred men could spend in a hundred lifetimes? So what if he had the adoration and loyalty of a mighty army, and could have anything in his realm that he desired even the least? He could have anything he wanted and was still not satisfied. All was vanity, all was false, and all was hopeless.

And we are all brought face to face, somehow, with our own personal, "All is vanity" revelation, so that we might all see that *all our righteousness is as filthy rags.*[217]

When I was first "saved," someone gave me tracts and literature that described what had happened to me. They told me that I had invited Jesus "into my heart," and that He was now on the throne of my heart. I remember a little diagram in one tract that first showed "self" on the throne of my life, but that now Jesus was on the inner throne of my life. It showed the little "s" (meaning self) off over to the side, still there, but no longer on the throne.

Actually, I don't think that picture's too far off, though I understood it little enough then. My "heart" was a vague picture to me, as was "Jesus coming to live in me." I really didn't have any idea what my "heart" was that Jesus came to live in, nor had I any idea of what it meant to have him "come in." Wonderfully, however, by grace we don't need the "understanding" at that point, just the willingness of heart (spirit) to invite him in, which we sense even in that early stage means the "death" of ourselves. Because for all of us, what we had to let go of, that day and that moment we finally, after all his knocking, "let him in," was some measure of our pride. Our "pride of self."

To admit our need, regardless of how it came to us in whatever situation, was to "let go" of ourselves, to admit, though without full consciousness of what we were admitting, that we need Another. We are not sufficient in ourselves. We've messed things up. We are lost from our true being. We are foundering in darkness, and don't know the way to go. We NEED help from above.

This is the opening the Spirit accomplishes within us, in our innermost depths, to prepare the ground for the Birth of the Newborn Babe in us, Who will grow up into the manifestation of the Life of God in us for the healing of the nations. Though we are dim in awareness of it, a great battle has occurred within us, and from beyond the deepest depths in our spirit, a great Champion has arisen inside us, Christ Jesus the Lord, who has urged and coaxed and warned and empowered from within, and has finally through hard warfare vanquished the hold of the usurper who has held us captive, has kicked out the moneychangers and scalawags who had taken residence in our house, and has changed the den of thieves into the House of Prayer for All Nations. We are a temple, both individually AND corporately, and He makes His Body by individually coming into His temples and taking up rightful residence in them, removing the Accuser of the Brethren from his attempt to create the abomination of desolation within us, and setting up again the Holy of Holies, wherein He eternally dwells between the Cherubims above the Mercy Seat, and we the High Priests who attend to the service in the Holy of Holies.

Once *"The Lord is in His Holy temple, let all the earth keep silence before Him"*[218] is established, i.e. He indwelling us, so that we are He in the world, then we are free to know "spirit" in right understanding, and right knowledge of "oneness."

If "spirit" is self, and God is Self and we are "selves," how is it then that there can be a "oneness" in "persons" as we describe it?

Here words fail us. We are two, yet One. We are One, yet two. He is in me; I am in Him. *"When you see Me, you see the Father." "My Father is greater than I."* What does this point us to? It points us to the Reality of God outside the realm of our intellect, above or beyond our understanding. *"I live, yet not I, but Christ."* How do we describe that in "earthly" terms?

I think the Sun's effect on the earth is the greatest natural demonstration of "union." The Sun shines its light from ninety-three million miles away, and the whole earth is given life by its light. Its light affects everything and causes ALL life on earth. The light of the sun affects chlorophyll in plants, which produces the oxygen we breathe. The light of the sun causes our weather patterns, the plants to grow, the animals to have water and habitat and food. The Sun is the life of the earth. Everything is some form of manifestation of sunlight. Yet what "contains" its light? It can only be experienced, benefited from, but not grasped and bottled and sold at the local market.

Another analogy is from the seventeenth century writer, Jacob Boehme. He continually referred to the picture of hot iron, heated in the blacksmith's fire. Take a piece of iron, and heat it in the fire until it's glowing red-hot. The picture Boehme portrayed was iron + fire, both remaining themselves, fire continuing to be fire, iron continuing to be iron, yet "ONE" in being red-hot iron.

Still another analogy is from the scriptures, the burning bush. Here was a bush on the side of a mountain, which was burning but was not consumed. This is a perfect picture of union with God. Because God's life exists in us not as a fire to consume, but as a fire to empower and enlighten. A fire to blaze in common everyday bushes. Us.

By this we see that God's Spirit, through the New Birth and His taking back His rightful throne in the center of our Being, "ones" Himself to us through the Cross of Jesus and His death and resurrection, not to consume us or to make us into something we're not, but rather to reveal Himself in us, and in that revelation of Himself, we find "our" true selves, where we'd always been hidden all along in Him, kept there waiting until the time was right to manifest the sons of God. It is in full manifestation of the One God that we see the full manifestation of the Sons, because He eternally exists to be the Fire of our lives, to be the heat in our iron, to be the Sun of Righteousness in the entire cosmos of our existence.

Now let me finally say this about "spirit." "Spirit" is not a "thing" that we can take apart, analyze, study and categorize. A certain amount we can handle, to get our terminology straight, but after a while it's like talking about swimming, when one needs actually to SWIM, if one is to know swimming.

When I say Spirit, both God and us, is "*I AM,*" absolute definitions fail us here. Mainly because how can one describe one's self? I look "out from" myself, but I can't look "back" at myself to identify my "self" as an object. (Who would it be looking "back at myself"?) "I" am always "subject" to myself. One can't escape one's "subjectivity." God is eternally "*I AM,*" -- subject, not object. Therefore

I cannot "objectively know myself." I can only BE myself. I live in Christ from an inner center of infinite depths that opens up from the heart of the Deity, a flow "out" of me, a flow "through me," a manifestation in the world AS me, but me as red-hot iron, me as a common bush aflame with living fire. Always a living union.

Sinful Flesh

The term "sinful flesh" is the problem here. As if flesh is the problem.

The problem is "sin" IN the flesh, making the flesh "sinful." Take the "sin" out, replace it with "righteousness," then you have righteous flesh. Flesh containing and expressing righteousness, which Romans Six so thoroughly says. Once slaves of indwelling sin, now slaves of indwelling righteousness.

We distinguish between the physical body and the condition of "sinful flesh." If the "flesh" itself (the body) is considered evil of itself, then we have one of the greatest falsehoods of all time, in which flesh is evil, and spirit is good, which is thinking that creeps into everything.

We have to understand that "sin" is not just some nebulous "principle," but is a person, the prince of the power of the air, in whose lap the whole world lies, even as righteousness is a Person. We were *by nature children of wrath*,[219] who did *the lusts of our father*.[220]

That is what John the Baptist meant when he said Jesus had come to lay an axe at the root of the tree. Mankind's problem is not inherent in his human makeup – spirit, soul, and body -- even in its "fallen" condition, but in "who" he received into him in eating the wrong tree. Who would he have received had he reached out to partake of the Tree of Life? Christ Himself, as fulfilled in Revelation. But it was not to be just yet. Adam (we) had necessarily to walk that road, so the way was barred for a time.

Jesus lays the axe at the "root of the tree," i.e. the "wrong tree," i.e. the "wrong master," by taking the person of sin into Himself. In the Cross He dies to "sin," for and as the whole human race. The sin spirit is cast out, and the Holy Spirit is poured out unto all flesh. (Of course, that redemption fulfills itself in us one by one as we're tapped on the shoulder or pursued by the "hound of heaven.")

I am speaking speculatively here, but I do believe He had the same "body" we all have, that of fallen Adam, from his mother Mary. The scriptures do not say he was born "sinless," but that He did not sin. If nothing else that shows that the power of the Holy Spirit in a person can keep him without sin in a fallen Adam body. For how else could He have not "sinned?"

We are not to be looking for a perfected humanity in itself but rather the whole of perfection resting in God Himself alone as the indwelling reality of the temples we are.

To repeat, "sinful flesh" is sin-indwelled, Satan-infected, flesh, with nothing whatsoever "wrong" with flesh of itself. Change owners, indwellers, vines to which we are attached, gods to indwell our temple, masters, and the SAME flesh and mind now is a *"member of righteousness."*[221] This means that in the Cross the human person – flesh – having now changed masters, is now the carrier of divinity in every part of its makeup – spirit, soul and body.

Romans Six is unequivocal. Sin is gone in the Cross. The Old Master is no longer our master! We have passed (not "will one day") from darkness unto Light, from Satan unto God.[222]

There is only One God. He is All in all and purposes all things after the counsel of His own Will. His own will, to quote William Law, is eternally a "Will to all goodness." He purposes in Himself to be outgoing Love, which He is in the Eternal Begetting of the Son and the outgoing of the Spirit.

The scriptures plainly say, however, that there is a false spirit, one who holds himself a "god," who is an "enemy," who seeks to kill and to destroy. We are aware of him and his devices, but we see him firmly in God's purposes, so in circumstances of life where I can truthfully say, "an enemy hath done this," I can also say that whatever the "enemy" meant for evil, God meant for God, and His GOOD purpose is seen in everything.

Now we are no longer part of that kingdom in the death and resurrection of Jesus, and what was formerly "sinful flesh" and corrupted "mind" has now become the dwelling place of the God who said, "*I will live in them and walk in them and be their God.*" We formerly walked after the self-for-self way of our old master. We were ignorant of it and it was not really with our full will or understanding that we were following his way, so well has he hidden himself. But now we are none of his. And we were never really "his" anyway. God just let him have us for a while to rough us up and train us very well in the negative, in order that we might have a right consciousness of the "Positive," and to insure the "safety" of His redeemed Sons, which we are.

Flesh and Spirit

Recently someone could not get past Paul's statement in Romans 7:18: *"For I know that in me (that is, in my flesh,) dwelleth no good thing."* In that person's mind, Paul's statement left him in a horrible state. A state of desiring the good things of God and yet because of a fatal flaw seemingly built into his humanity, he could never hope to have those good things in this life. In other words, to him, *"no good thing in me,"* meant that, as long as he was in this life, he would continue to be a "sinful" or "wrong" sort of person in some integral part of himself. He would never be able to get past that. That and the overriding sense of not only being "wrong," but also it being his own fault that he is "wrong" (as if there was something he could do about it).

And in one way or another, using different words but meaning more or less the same thing, most people live in some reality like that. Call it "two natures," "lower self/ higher self," "human nature/divine nature," but built into the belief-system of most people is some means whereby we justify and explain our seeming constant shortcomings and faults to ourselves and to others by saying, "Hey, I'm not perfect! I make mistakes, and will continue to do so. I'm only human."

In my early Christian experience I was taught that two passages, Genesis 6:5, *"Every imagination of the thoughts of [man's] heart is only evil continually,"* and Jeremiah 17:9, *"The heart is deceitful above all things, and desperately wicked: who can know it?"* were concurrent realities with my new life in Christ. That is, even though I had been born again, so I was taught, nonetheless my heart was still only evil continually and desperately wicked. That was the justification in my situation then to have a "shepherd," or minister above me to keep me "safe."

That left me in the same place as the man who interpreted, *"in me dwelleth no good thing,"* to mean the same (result-wise) as having an evil heart. Above all things, I could not trust myself. Of all the creatures on the face of the earth, I held myself in the highest suspicion, because at any time I could be deceiving myself. It made everything suspect. And that isn't freedom, but a horrific bondage.

Actually, Paul's *"no good thing in me,"* and the two passages from Genesis and Jeremiah are technically not talking about the same thing. But the point I am making is that in experience they seemed to be the same. Our view is that we have this "wild untrustworthy" part of ourselves, called "the flesh," that any given moment can run amok, and does most of the time. We know we should have control but we just can't seem to ever gain the upper hand, since "the flesh" is always about two steps ahead. So we just do our best and keep apologizing for it after the fact to whomever it happens to mow down as it plows from one crooked furrow to another. Or maybe we just have the nagging sense that seems to hang under every moment, that we are incomplete somehow, never quite what we should be or could be, and always with the sense of never having done enough or always needing to do more. We know that if we were better, then God would bless us more, fill us more, love through us more. And for most of us the "better" is as elusive as wind.

The answer to this is very good news indeed.

The first very good news is that in Christ my heart is no longer wicked.

It seems so basic, yet tragically missed by many of us.

The new birth is simply the regaining of the citadel of the human heart (spirit) by its original builder and Source, the Living God, by Christ's conquering of the devil who had usurped that inner sanctuary of our heart. He had hiddenly dwelled there as a deceiver since Adam, infecting us with his own wrath, rebellion, selfishness and pride, through the body of sin he created in us and which manifests out of us as a tree of judgment, exclusiveness, self-protection, self-promotion, selfish need and many other things.

What had before been the harmony of nature, the devil fractured into a million broken pieces in our consciousness. By that fracture the image of God was broken in us and in its place has come a veiled image of selfish grasping that is the history of the world, both personal and universal. It is lunacy at its core, but on which is placed a veneer of respectability and progress, so that the whole world can continually assuage itself over its good deeds and caring for mankind, while insanity and madness rage mockingly in the background.

But the new birth changes that in individuals and renews the whole world. The image of God, fallen almost into ruin, is reawakened in us when Jesus comes to dwell in us in the new birth. The ruined landscape, the fields lying fallow, the fences broken and the wells almost dry -- the landscape of our old lives -- now belongs to Him, and not to the old master who had driven it all into degradation.

We have received a new heart in the New Testament, in the new birth of Christ in us. He is now our heart. Our innermost self. Therefore the "wicked heart" that the Bible says I had was not just "me" having a wicked heart, but the <u>devil in my heart</u>. The "wickedness" in my heart, the "evil imagination," did not originate in my humanity, in my "self," but was of the *"prince of the power of the air"* who works "in" the children of disobedience.[223]

The "new heart" given us in salvation[224] is none other than Christ come to dwell in our hearts through faith in Him. CHRIST HIMSELF is our new heart! (Simple words -- the deepest truth there is!)

The former master we served unknowingly, Satan, whose deeds we did and thoughts we believed, has been cast out. He was the "old" wicked heart. We had been all our lives unwitting (or maybe very willingly) servants of unrighteousness, of sin, of selfishness to the core. The "old man" was the union between ourselves and the false spirit of unrighteousness, who usurped the temple of God in our innermost sanctuary, causing us to fulfill "his lusts," while all the time deceiving us into thinking we were just ourselves alone functioning in life, doing good and evil, right and wrong.

That's all the "old man" is. The old union, between the human self and the satanic spirit of error, is broken permanently in the new birth. Can we get this straight? People tend to think that the "old man" is some other part of us, some wayward beast in us, which we still have to contend with all the days of this life. But that is not true. The "old man" has no reality except in the way lies have reality. They have some validity to those who believe them. But if you have been born again of God, then you are no longer the "old man." The old man died! Read Romans Six.

You no longer have a wicked heart. Your heart is no longer evil continuously in its imaginations, because the One who is now your heart has only love as His imagination. All <u>His</u> imaginings are stirrings toward life and hope. And His imaginings are now the imaginings of YOUR heart, since He dwells there. You have become His temple. You are a branch that sprouts from the True Vine. You are a member of His body. Physically, organically, spiritually, emotionally, <u>literally</u> you are the house of His dwelling, the temple in which He shows His glory to the world. This is the absolute literal truth. Believest thou this?

In order for the temple of our humanity to be cleansed, rid of the moneychangers and thieves, made again into a house of prayer by God dwelling in us, the uncleanness had to be cast out. There is only room in the center of our being for one god, either the God of Love or the false god of wrath and selfishness. Both cannot dwell there. That's why it is plain in the New Testament that we died with Him in the Cross, that He was made the "sin" that we ourselves had become by taking the spirit of error who inhabited all humanity into Himself in His death, and thus separating humanity from its false king forever. From that death He rose again by the Holy Spirit who fills the newly cleansed temple of humanity with the fullness of God, enacted in us one at a time as we each come to faith.

A new heart, a new life, a new mind, all are in Him in the new birth. We are a "completely new creation." "Behold, I make all things new."

Do we see the shift in consciousness here? From a mindset that there is something wicked about ourselves, to simply believing in Christ, in us? The New Testament gives us permission to say adieu to the old man, good-bye forever, and to rise in newness and abundance of life, which is not about bondage and fear, but about love, truth, righteousness and holiness that springs out of an eternal well of living water we find within ourselves, which is Christ.

From out of our deepest center, our "heart," Christ comes, the Eternal Son, who is the wellspring out of the depths of the Father, wherein are found all the treasures of wisdom and knowledge -- a wisdom and knowledge not of the flesh, not of this world, but out of the mystery of God.

1 Corinthians 6:17 states possibly the most profound truth about the new birth found in the whole of scripture. Short and sweet, the verse says simply: *"He that is joined unto the Lord is one spirit."* It is the whole truth in the most concise of nutshells -- God and you by the new birth are now joined as one person, one heart, and one spirit. You can't be more intimately joined with a person than that. Sexual union between lovers is only a pale representation, because after the fulfillment and bliss we are always left with two, but with God we are one. What sex only points to in the physical, two becoming one, union with God accomplishes; two ARE one. The complete union between persons, so that they are now one person. So it is in passion, intimacy, fear, trembling, hope, vision, in tears and love, that God and we are One, He having taken up dwelling in our temple, He clothing Himself with us as we are raised in our faith-awareness to, *"I live, yet not I, but Christ liveth in me, and the life I live in the flesh I live by the faith of the Son of God, who loved me, and gave Himself for me."*[225]

Paul's statement, *"in me dwelleth no good thing,"* is therefore not a negative statement about our human condition. It is said in the same sense in which Jesus replied to the man who called him "Good master":

"Why callest thou me good. There is none good, but one, God."[226]

If the first in-depth lesson of our new birth is that we have a completely new heart/spirit/mind/law within us, then the second in-depth further lesson is what we learn here.

Because we are immediately faced, once we know we have been born again, with now going about to establish our own righteousness as a born-again person, as we attempted to establish our own righteousness in our prior life. We want to be like Christ, to live a holy life, to love others -- all the things we know we are supposed to do and be. We are told we should be those things, and we think we can, especially now that we have "God's help."

The "new heart" in us produces an earnestness after the things of God. We *delight in the law of God after the inner man,* as Paul said of himself in Romans Seven.

But Paul ran into a problem, as does every person of God, in that in trying to accomplish God's will, he seemed to find an opposite principle working: that is, the more he tried to do God's will, the more he seemed to fail. And not only fail, but also he found himself doing the very things he knew he shouldn't be doing, thinking things he knew he shouldn't be thinking.

"What gives?" Paul asks. "I love God, want to please him, try my best, and fall flat on my face. I seem a hypocrite. I know I'm born again. The 'old man' I was has been crucified in the Cross of Jesus, and I have risen with Him into newness of Life. So why can't I now live the way I believe God wants me to live?"

Because even more fundamental than finding out how our heart has changed, is finding out who we really are and how we operate. And God's way of letting us find out who we are, is to first give us a good dose of who we are not.

We are born as who we're not. Since Adam all humanity has been born with devil-infected mind and heart, producing the selfishness, lust and greed that drives all human society. Every person in this world is deceived about who we are, and every one of us believes from birth the devil's chief lie, the "lie of independent self," which stated simply just means self thinking and self believing itself to be its own god, its own righteousness or its own evil, its own strength or its own weakness, its own power or its own impotence. And that's the reality we, the whole human race, live in from birth, and it has been so throughout the entire course of our history.

But that is who we are not. Every man born into the world is an image of God, meant to reflect God. Christ is the light that lights every man who comes into the world. Who we all really are, is HE. There is no person, anywhere, who is not God in expression, because God is the Only Self-Existent Person there is. Everyone else, human or angel, derives his "personhood" out of the Person of God.

The lie, which as I said above can produce its own false reality, says that there are others gods besides God, and that you and I are those other gods. (*"Thou shalt have no other gods before me."*) The lie of independent self says that I have my own life, my own will, my own thinking, my own desires, my own power, my own heart, my my my my my my my!!!! The lie of independent self makes me a person sufficient in myself. I may want to express my "independence" by trying to "serve God and do good," or

I may want to express my independence by searing my conscience and becoming a conscious taker from others. Either way, either lifestyle is predicated on a lie of colossal proportions.

And it's very subtle, this "lie." As a Spirit-filled believer, a God-person, the "lie" deceives me into thinking I can accomplish God's will -- with God's help of course, but still it's "me" putting forth the effort, coming up with the desire, making the "choice," and following through to the end. When Moses presented the children of Israel with the Law, they all said in unison, "All that the Lord has spoken we will do."

And we know the result of that. And it's the same result with us when we are like the children of Israel, who still had a consciousness of flesh, i.e. according to the lie of independence. In that deception we believe, just like the children of Israel before us, that "we" can fulfill God's law, that "we" can accomplish

God's will, and if we were just a little more disciplined, a little more reverent, a little more prayerful, we would have the whole thing knocked. And our result is the same as theirs. We fare no better than they. They fell flat on their faces and so do we.

This is all according to plan.

First of all, we are MEANT to live in the lie. It is the necessary backdrop to coming to the knowledge of the truth.

Secondly, we are MEANT to think we can live God's life and accomplish God's will. It's the only thing that will break the back of the monster that the spirit of error has created in us. The spirit of error has done us a good turn, in making us conscious of ourselves as selves. But in so doing he created this horrible selfish little monster, that always has to have its own way, its own rights protected, its territory defended, and its reputation upheld. He gives us this monster to be our own selves, which in our deception we put on everyday thinking this is who we are.

For reasons that God knows, He does not immediately destroy this false sense of self in our new birth. Instead He lets us walk on a while, ignorant of the body of sin that still holds us in our consciousness (even though no longer in our heart), in order that we might FAIL!

And fail we do. It doesn't really matter how the failure manifests. That isn't the point. The point is that at some juncture, we come up against a brick wall, as Paul did with his demon "covetousness," and all the constructs we had built to protect and hold up our "self" are kicked out, and down we go.

Now we are conditioned for the final revelation about ourselves, which is really twofold as Paul outlined in Romans Seven. Paul first realizes that when he does evil, and he has not willed it, but instead has "willed" the law of God in his inward man, it is not he, Paul, who does the evil. He has discovered a principle, that when he attempts, in his consciousness of independence, to "do righteousness," he instead does the opposite. In other words, he discovers that when he "tries" to do good, he does evil instead.[227]

How come? Why would that be? It doesn't seem fair!

It's very simple, really, once you come onto the other side of things. "Self-effort," "trying" from the false sense of ourselves, etc., are all still offshoots of the lie of independent self, which says WE ourselves can be God. (Maybe this thought-pattern doesn't actually dare to believe it is God conceptually, but by default it does, because it thinks it can produce the "works" of God – holiness, righteousness, goodness, love, etc.) But this lie is the devil's playground, his bailiwick, and his ball game. He invented it, and has refined it a million-fold over the eons of time he's had to work on it. It is the "accursed thing." So, we discover as children of God, that when we play in the devil's playground with his toys, we are once again temporarily back on his turf, where he says what goes on.

In other words, self-effort, i.e. effort from the false sense of myself as someone separate from God trying to be like God or do His will, is really Satan, the devil, masquerading himself in the false sense of myself as independent. Or, as Paul puts it in Romans Seven, *"it is no longer I that do it, but sin that dwelleth in me."* (Understand here, without our going into too great detail, that when Paul speaks of sin dwelling "in my flesh", he is not speaking of his physical body or his supposed "fallen nature," but rather in the false sense of independence and separation that deceives the whole human race. So when Paul talks about "sin" dwelling in his flesh, he is not describing a physical locality but rather a mindset, a consciousness. A mindset of independence, or supposed self-sufficiency.)

So the first great discovery here, as stated above, is that when he "tries" or "would" do good, evil comes. His second great discovery is that "in me dwelleth no good thing."

As I said above, that is exactly in the same sense as when Jesus said, *"Why callest thou me good?"* Once we have discovered that not only does the evil not originate from us, but from the father of lies, and then have further discovered that even our attempts to do good produce evil, which also comes from the father of lies, we are then ready for the final revelation of revelations.

That is this: having now discovered no power of myself to do either evil OR good, I am ready to be what consciously what I have been always unconsciously -- a vessel for another.

My humanity (spirit, soul, body) has been the devil's beast of burden in my ignorance and separation from God. I didn't know it, even when I was cooperating with it. But like every other human on the face of the earth, I have been the vessel of wrath, the temple of the false god, walking in the pride of life and the lusts of this world. But, as I have discovered now in Romans Seven, it wasn't "just me," but the usurper, the liar, IN me.

Now, in Christ, I see, and this IS IT, THE revelation of all revelations -- in finding that "*in me dwelleth no good thing*," in that emptiness, CHRIST manifests Himself. God is a JEALOUS God, He says over and over, and that simply means that He will share His glory with no one, and no flesh shall enter His presence. Rather than being something negative or disappointing, now to find that "*in me dwelleth no good thing*," is now WONDERFUL NEWS, JOYOUS NEWS, because the government has been taken from my shoulders, the government of my life and that of the whole universe, and put on the shoulders of the ONLY ONE who can handle the burden: Christ Jesus, Lord of Lords and King of Kings.

How wonderful it is to say that all goodness, all holiness, all righteousness, all power, and all glory, reside in God Alone, and only in Him. And nothing in me.

Hallelujah! What freedom! What love!

To discover that my "own" weakness and emptiness is the exact prerequisite for the Life of God to live in me and to manifest in the world is the most wonderful news ever!!!!

So now without reservation I can say, like Paul, that *"no good thing dwelleth in me,"* and at the same time say, *"God is mighty in me toward the Gentiles."*[228] Why -- because in coming to the place of complete emptiness and "no-self" before the Lord, we are then ready to move into the stage where we are "mighty selves" in Him who accomplish all His will.

Cleansing the Temple

In the Gospel of John, after the wedding at Cana in Galilee, Jesus goes up to the Passover in Jerusalem. When He witnesses the scene at the Temple, the buying, selling, bartering and haggling, looking to see the house of prayer, He sees that it has become instead a bazaar. Overcome with anger at the abomination, gentle Jesus meek and mild makes a whip out of ropes, and starts running through the place like a madman, turning over tables, yelling at people, whipping people. ***"Take these things hence!"***[229] He shouts as he overturns one man's table, scattering coins and paraphernalia in its wake. ***"My father's house shall be called a house of prayer, but ye have made it a den of thieves!"***[230]

The Pharisees asked Him for a sign, which would prove He had the authority to do what He did. He said, *"Destroy this temple, and in three days I will raise it up."*[231]

John adds, *"He spake of the temple of His body."*[232]

We all know what He was talking about, since we've all read this many times. We know that His opponents didn't understand what He was talking about but we do, since we know He rose from the dead. That's what He was talking about. We learned it in Sunday School.

But He meant even more than that. Jesus was the real temple of God, not some stone building constructed my man. He was the "place" where God dwelled and showed His glory. And Jesus was a man, meaning that God had taken residence in a <u>human being</u>. God had chosen to dwell in His fullness in a man. And Jesus came to be the new man. He was the "Second Adam," the start of a new heavenly race of men, even as the First Adam had been the start of the earthly race. He was the Son of God, the only begotten of the Father, manifest in physical flesh, who had come to restore the kingdom of God, which is not a physical kingdom, but instead is the realm of the heart, the spirit, to bring mankind out of the slavery of the king of Egypt into the liberty of the sons of God, by the restoration of God's presence in the inner sanctuary of man's most intimate center.

When Jesus threw the moneychangers out of the temple, He was doing far more than making a statement about selling raffle tickets in the church building. He was demonstrating what He was going to accomplish with the *"baptism He had to be baptized with."*[233] He had come to lay the axe to the root of the Tree. He had come to sweep the temple of mankind clean of the usurper. The temple of man had become a "den of thieves," because the wicked one whispered in everybody's ears and we all listened and let him move in.

He rid the temple of the pack of thieves so that He could come back and hear, *"Blessed is He Who comes in the name of the Lord."*[234] He had come to fulfill the prophecy:

Behold, the days come.... I will put my law in their inward parts, and write it in their hearts; and will be their God, and they shall be my people. And they shall teach no more every man his neighbour, and every man his brother, saying, Know the LORD: for they shall all know me, from the least of them unto the greatest of them, saith the LORD: for I will forgive their iniquity, and I will remember their sin no more.[235]

Before Jesus left the apostles, He told them everything at the Last Supper. *"I am my Father are One,"* He says.

"When you see Me you see the Father." God has glorified Jesus with the glory of His own self, so that the Father and Jesus the Son are One. There is a Father and there is a Son, and they are One.

But He goes further. More is being restored in the kingdom of God than a political change in the government. It's a change of country. A change of everything. A passage from darkness to light. Jesus says the *"glory which thou gavest me I have given them, that they may be one, even as we are one, I in them, and thou in me."*[236] In that one statement of Jesus at the Last Supper, we cannot fail to see union with God as the purpose of the New Birth from above. We are to "be one, even as [Father and Son] are one." That is the power of God. The <u>SAME</u> union reality that exists in the Godhead, so that they are each other and yet themselves, is the same union reality that envelops us in the resurrection of the Lord Jesus!

"And this is life eternal, that they might know thee the only true God, and Jesus Christ, whom thou hast sent.... And now, O Father, glorify thou me with thine own self with the glory which I had with thee before the world was.... And the glory which thou gavest me I have given them; that they may be one, even as we are one: I in them, and thou in me, that they may be made perfect in one."[237]

Jesus came to declare the Father, which was consummated when He gave Himself up to death, as the Father's ultimate love-act to bring life out of death. He came to lead captivity captive, and to give gifts unto men. He came to lift us up into "heavenly places," and lovingly sit us down right beside Him in the throne of glory, where

He ever lives as a Lamb slain, and we with Him, even while we live in the earth.

By His death He slew the enmity, the hold of the false king. He cleansed the temple, to make it a fit dwelling for His Father. As Moses raised a serpent on a pole in the wilderness,[238] and all who looked at it were healed, Jesus took the serpent into Himself while raised on a pole, and submitted unto death.[239]

In unimaginable places in eternity something must certainly have transacted during those three earthly days of His lying in His tomb. Some great spiritual cataclysm occurred, because when He ascended from the depths of the *"lower parts of the earth,"*[240] Paul says, He *"led captivity captive."*[241] Paul goes on to say that from the lowest parts of the earth He then ascended up on high, so that He might fill <u>all things</u>. He went from the lowest depths of Hell to the Highest heights of Heaven to fill all with the fullness of Himself in His death and resurrection. ALL OF IT!

In the simplest of terms, in the Cross -- His death and resurrection -- Jesus destroyed in us the kingdom of the devil, expelled the usurper out of the inner sanctuary of our deepest selves, and by the entrance of His Spirit He has restored the temple of our human selves into the dwelling place of God, a "house of prayer." What was formerly a den of thieves has now become the glory of God. Emmanuel is now you and I!

And the further mystery is that He dwells within us as simply our plain old human selves. As who we are in this present moment. Our face is the face of Christ in the world. Our hands are His hands. Our eyes are His eyes.

Union is the goal of the thirsty soul. It is not the end, really only the beginning, but union with God in Christ is the foundation of everything.

Union is not some goal attained by years spent in a monastery, or by years and years of ministry or missionary service, or by night after night after night spent on our knees in prayer. It is not a work of our own, and cannot be "attained." You can't do one thing to "get it."

Union simply IS. We ARE "One" with God in Christ, by virtue of the death and resurrection of Christ Jesus. When Paul wrote, "*I am crucified with Christ, nevertheless I live, yet not I, but Christ liveth within me,*" he wrote it not merely for himself, as if he was some holier person than everybody else, but as the true state of all who have been born from above.

How did Paul get there? He told us, a thousand times over. "*The just shall live by faith.*" "*And Abraham believed in the Lord, and he counted it unto him as righteousness.*"

There is no "attaining" union. Believe on Him. He is your Real True Self. "*I am the Lord and there is no other.*"[242]

He that cometh to God must believe that He is, and that He is a rewarder of them that diligently seek Him.[243]

There remaineth therefore a rest to the people of God. For he that is entered into his rest, he also hath ceased from his own works, as God did from his.[244]

There is only one entrance into the things of God – the way of faith. Yet as with so many other things, we often have difficulty knowing exactly what faith is and how it works.

When the Living God was stirring my life to bring me to Himself when I was a young man, I initially looked into systems that gave definite formulas, specific things you could do or ways to behave to become closer to the Truth. It seemed easy enough. Meditate. Do yoga exercises. Eat the right foods. Align my thoughts to higher things.

There was a sense in which it "worked," for a while. I seemed calmer. I seemed to have found some degree of peace. I began to "see spiritual things." It seemed the more I practiced meditation and right diet and right thoughts the more peaceful I felt and the more serene I could "act." One day, however, my roommate's girlfriend told me off. She told me I was out for myself as much as anybody else. She wasn't fooled by my "spiritual" guise. Of course, I was aghast. But even more, I was unraveled, because I realized she was right. All the yoga exercises, meditation, right foods, and all the thought control I'd been practicing I knew had not broken the stranglehold in my inner being of my selfish self.

So I battened down the hatches and renewed my efforts with greater fervor. I was DETERMINED to break the hold, somehow, some way. Along the way, a young man with a penetrating witness to the Living Jesus Christ came across my path, and told me in a way I could not ignore that the only way to God was through faith in Jesus Christ, and not through my own efforts. Only by receiving Him, he said, and not by my yoga, or my knowledge, or my philosophy, could I come to know God and Truth.

I was undone once again, because even though I somehow knew inwardly he spoke truth for me, still I could not give up the idea that "I" must do something. "I" must attain. "I" must become. To simply "receive" was TOO EASY! How could that be?

I still had a few more months left in me of kicking around in my own efforts before the Lord was finally able to corner me with my own futility, my own utter inability to know, do or be anything. It was in the darkest moment of that realized futility, that unbeknownst to me, I spoke a "word of faith."

I'd never heard the term before that I recall, so it was strictly something from the heart. But in the depths of utter darkness, when I had fallen in myself into complete despair of ever coming to God, when I couldn't see God, couldn't hear God, couldn't fathom God, and didn't even BELIEVE (in my mind) in God, I TOLD GOD I believed in Him. And that even though I could not rationally justify it, I would believe in His Son Jesus.

I didn't see angels, hear voices, experience a great flood of light, or anything particularly dramatic. From that moment, however, I began to know Jesus my Savior and God my Father. Completely inexplicably, and coming out of nowhere I'd ever been before.

That is the way of faith. It is not a mental exercise, to train our minds to believe certain things. Faith is simply receiving what is there. We do not "understand" going in. We do not at first "see" (visibly) the "thing" faith says is ours.

Consider a marriage ceremony. Two people have courted, and at some point have decided they would like to get married. That point where the proposal is made and accepted is the first "word of faith" they speak, which gets the ball rolling toward the marriage ceremony. Finally the day comes. Everybody dresses in their finest, the groom and his company awaiting the bride at the front of the church, the bride and her train processing to join the groom and the minister at the altar. The minister reads the ceremony, and finally at the climax of the service, the vows are recited, the "I do's" said, and the minister pronounces them husband and wife.

They are married. Now, they may have fifty or more years to work it out, and many things will be settled and ironed out in those years, but they won't be any more married fifty years after the ceremony than they were the day they said their vows – their "word of faith," that they are married. Once they made the proclamation in the sight of God and the witnesses in the Church, by their WORD they were truly married.

It is with that same simplicity that we recognize and enter into our "union" with God, our "rest." Paul said it for us, and we need only to repeat it with him and believe that the word he spoke about himself applies also to us, because we are no different from Paul.

"I am crucified with Christ," Paul first says. I have "died" in Christ's death. The "old me" is gone. Dead.

"Nevertheless I live," he goes on to say. Wait a minute, Paul is saying. I DID die; I gave it all up, but wait a minute, I'M LIVING. How can that be?

"Yet not I, but Christ liveth in me." Paul is saying the deepest truth in the scripture here. It is NO LONGER I, but CHRIST LIVING – where??? – IN ME!!!!!

This is where faith takes hold, because these are facts with no visible evidence. I may look exactly the opposite from what I think Christ would look like. Yet here in the scriptures the word is welling up within me to believe what Paul says, despite what I seem to myself to be.

Our "word of faith" in this instance is to say about ourselves what God says about us – that it is no longer "we" living, but Christ living in us. We believe it and say it, in the face of what appears to be completely the opposite, and trust GOD that it is true, with the mind of father Abraham, who *"called things which be not as though they were."*[245]

It does not require great understanding, or comprehension of all the subtleties of the deepest teachings, in order to enter into the rest of union with God, where God does all and we nothing, as Jesus said of Himself in John 8:28. Just say it. He does all the rest.

"I and my Father are One."[246]

Hearts of Flesh – "As the waters cover the sea"

In the beginning of this book, and indeed throughout it, we have spoken about experiencing no hope, despair, failure and barrenness in some sense as prerequisites to a "heart of flesh." Truly, it is by experiencing and living life in all its sweets and bitters, positives and negatives, that we discover and live the Divine within it, and are found to be fully "human."

And now having found God in love in the midst of everything there is, how does our world look to us now, and what purpose do we have in living in it?

Years ago, when I was a very young man, one night I found myself standing at the edge of a high plateau in the eastern foothills of the Rocky Mountains in Colorado. It was high summer just after dusk, and looking out eastward into the unending sea that is the Great Plains, I was overcome with the nearness and vastness of the infinite landscape in front of me, that even in its infinity was framed and overshadowed by the Big Sky all around. The stars were so real and vibrating so close by, that a nighttime military map exercise became a moment transfigured in starlight forever. I didn't "know Him" yet, but there He was, bigger than life anyway.

A thousand other such stories I could tell, and I think most of us, if we thought about it, could tell similar stories. Different places. Different facets. But there is no one on earth who is without epiphanies, without glimpses of God here and there.

By grace and mercy those epiphanies have come up like sprouting seeds in our lives, testifying to truth and love and sometimes being demanding of us because in an epiphany, we see something miraculous, something "higher" than ourselves, and it holds tight to us like an ideal we know is true but is perhaps for a long time seemingly out of reach.

But we can't let it go. We've seen something, even if nobody else believes it, and though maybe ethereal, impractical, illogical and impossible, especially to someone such as ourselves, embarrassment be damned anyway and we plow on like big bulls in little china shops with the expected results.

But the vision grows. And with the expanding vision the heart bursts out of its cavity. Because now we know the vision is far vaster than we first thought, and we see that love exceeds all boundaries and is without any limitation.

And this now is the fullness flowing out of our hearts and minds and affecting everyone around us with light and glory, just as the stars shine so elegantly and vibrantly in the Colorado sky.

The stars shine; the rain falls; the heart bursts, and out of it the love of God fills everything. In all the valleys and over all the hills. As the waters cover the sea.

Postscript

Almost everything in the preceding articles is livingly based on scriptural understandings that I learned first from the books, and then even more from the life of the person who taught them to me by being them in front of me. He was the missionary, Christian leader and writer, Norman Grubb, who when asked by a friend in my presence if he'd ever "been to the Holy Land," replied (in his proper Cambridge English), "My dear, I AM the Holy Land."[247]

Later on, what began as principles I learned from Norman failed, and I attempted to forget it all for years. No could do, however, because though I threw away the syllabus for a long time, the "law" of how to believe and live in union with God, one day I saw the "Royal Law of Liberty" in a new light, it having come up completely of Itself. Even more surprisingly (because I was no longer looking for it), in my loss, weakness, and even forgetfulness of it, it (the Living God) suddenly by grace became the Inner Rod of Iron I had believed He was so long before and which for years had seemed so elusive to attain.

And that Rod of Iron did not come as rigid engravings in stone tablets, but as Emmanuel (Christ in me) in a heart of flesh.

Endnotes

1   Col 1:26,27
2   2 Cor 3:3, Ez 11:19
3   1 Sam 3:10
4   2 Cor 6:16
5   1 Cor 6:17
6   John 4:14
7   (Hint: "Christ living in me")
8   Ps 2:7
9   Ex 20:3
10   2 Tim 2:13
11   Col 3:3,4; 2 Cor 3:5
12   Gal 4:19
13   Luke 1:38
14   2 Cor 6:16
15   "Actual substance" means it is real, that it is <u>really</u> there.
16   Phil 1:6
17   Gen 15:6
18   Gen 16:12
19   1 Sam 10:7
20   Gen 15:5,6
21   Gal 3:16
22   John 8:56
23   Ps 19:1
24   Col 1:26
25   Gen 15:2
26   Rom 8:20
27   2 Kings 7
28   Ps 1:3
29   1 John 4:2,3
30   Ps 139:17
31   Ps 139:16

32 Col 1:17

33 Rev 21:3

34 1 Cor 15:47

35 Gal 2:20

36 2 Cor 4:7

37 Is 61:1,2

38 Ps 118:23

39 2 Cor 3:18

40 Col 1:17; Heb 1:2,3; John 1:3

41 Mark 12:27

42 2 Tim 1:12

43 Ps 32:2a

44 John 3:8

45 Num 11:29

46 1 John 4:12

47 Ps 27:10

48 Luke 14:33

49 Matt 9:29

50 Mark 11:24

51 Mark 11:23

52 Ps 42:3

53 Is 11:9

54 Rev 1:6

55 Rom 3:4

56 Matt 26:26

57 Matt 3:10,11

58 2 Cor 5:21

59 Lev 16

60 Matt 22:42-45

61 Eph 4:10

62 Num 13:33

63 Heb 2:6-11

64 Heb 10

65 Heb 10:10

66 Heb 10:14

67 Heb 7:25
68 John 4:34
69 Col 1:24
70 Heb 9:14; 10:2
71 Ps 16:10
72 John 12:24
73 John 10:30
74 1 Cor 1:29
75 Rom 3:20
76 Ps 119:105
77 Gen 22:4
78 Gen 22:5
79 Gen 22:8
80 Gen 22:18
81 Ps 118:17
82 Ps 16:10
83 Eph 1:11
84 Gen 22:8
85 Ps 73:25,26
86 Col 1:17; John 1:1
87 Acts 17:28
88 Rev 10:6
89 2 Cor 5:4
90 I would also say that the Eternal Self IS our very foundational self, and that there is no other. But the language is too strong and such a notion ultimately unsafe until the cherubim's sword has done its work. The angel bars the way to the Tree of Life until it is safe to eat from the Tree. To eat from the Tree of oneness with God means the complete freedom of the created self in wholeness and self-affirmation, and if there is no true Cross there, what rises is a monster. So the true way is barred until Christ is born in us, but anyone can find the false way if they wish.

91   Is 6:8
92   Matt 4:19
93   Ps 118:24
94   Ps 31:15
95   Gal 4:19
96   Heb 4:16
97   Eph 5:14
98   Matt 14:31
99   Ps 4:7
100 Is 64:8
101 Col 2:14
102 Mark 8:35
103 Is 55:1
104 Is 6:5
105 Rev 4:11
106 *Is* 8:2
107 John 5:46
108 Rev 7:17; 13:8
109 Luke 2:25-27; Mark 12:36; Acts 1:16; Ezek 2:1,2
110 Gal 3:19
111 Rom 8:20
112 Heb 13:8
113 Gen 6:8
114 Hab 2:20
115 Joel 2:28, 29
116 John 14:17
117 Rev 21:3
118 Heb 7:25
119 Matt 16:17
120 Matt 1:20
121 Eph 4:15
122 Rev 21:5
123 Rev 21:1
124 Matt 24:27
125 John 8:36

126 2 Cor 5:17
127 Luke 15:31
128 John 5:6
129 2 Cor 6:2
130 Mark 4:28
131 Rom 10:8
132 Ps 112:4
133 Ps 127:1
134 Is 40:31
135 Is 55:1
136 Eph 1:11
137 Rom 8:20
138 Job 1:8
139 Job 1:21
140 Job 13:15
141 John 19:11
142 Rom 8:21
143 Rom 9
144 John 14:30
145 Eph 4:27
146 Acts 26:18
147 1 Cor 15:55,57
148 Eph 3:30
149 Rom 8:26,27
150 Eph 3:17
151 Eph 3:18,19
152 Gen 41:38
153 1 Cor 15:21,22
154 Lk 1:35
155 Matt 16:19
156 Matt 18:3
157 John 17:5
158 1 Cor 4:7
159 Matt 7:21
160 1 Pet 1:3

161 Rev 21:4
162 Luke 10:30-37
163 Matt 25:40
164 James 1:27
165 I Cor 13:5
166 Jude 1:23
167 Rom 8:9
168 John 5:6
169 1 Cor 2:2
170 Ps 118:17
171 Ps 32:2
172 John 15:5
173 2 Cor 3:5
174 2 Cor 5:19
175 Mark 1:11
176 Ps 42:1
177 Rom 9:13
178 Rom 9:20
179 John 4:34
180 Matt 24:40
181 Ps 91:7
182 Rom 6:1
183 Num 23:21
184 2 Cor 6:16
185 Acts 17:28
186 Ps 100:3
187 Acts 10:38
188 John 16:33
189 I am not disallowing the possibility of sinning. I am simply not restating the obvious, especially since Moses is well represented wherever we go. We may come out of Moses if we wish by finding the God-given faith-consciousness of continual righteousness through Christ in us. In other words, being "righteous-minded,"(Christ-minded) instead of "sin-

minded" (Law-minded).

190 Gal 2:8; John 7:38
191 John 8:7
192 Luke 23:43
193 "Seeing a person as Christ" is not a dogma or a law, but a revelation.
194 John 1:12
195 1 Cor 6:17
196 Heb 4:3
197 Matt 5:8
198 Is 6:3
199 Col 3:3
200 1 John 3:2
201 Gal 2:20
202 Ps 121:4
203 Gal 1:15,16
204 Rev 3:30
205 Ps 18:26
206 Gen 50:20
207 John 6:29
208 Ps 79:5
209 Ps 69:5
210 2 Cor 4:10
211 John 4:24
212 Heb 12:9
213 Prov 20:27
214 John 1:9
215 Gen 2:7
216 Ecc 1:2
217 Is 64:6
218 Hab 2:20
219 Eph 2:3
220 John 8:44
221 Rom Chap 6
222 Acts 26:18; 2 Cor 6:14,15; Eph 2:2,3; John 8:44; 1

John 5:19
223 Eph 2:2
224 Ez 36:26
225 Gal 2:20
226 Mark 10:18
227 Rom 7:15-25
228 Gal 2:8
229 John 2:16
230 Matt 21:13
231 John 2:19
232 John 2:21
233 Mark 10:38
234 Matt 23:39
235 Jer 31:31-34
236 John 17:22
237 John 17:3,5,22,23
238 Num 21
239 John 3:14
240 Eph 4:9
241 Eph 4:8
242 Is 45:6
243 Heb 11:6
244 Heb 4:9,10
245 Rom 4:17
246 John 10:30
247 Norman wrote many books and articles in his seventy years career, too many to list. But the following list contains my favorites: C.T. Studd, Rees Howells, Intercessor, The Law of Faith, The Deep Things of God, God Unlimited, The Spontaneous You, Who Am I and Yes I Am. I highly recommend them, since he laid out in an easily understood, systematic fashion, the depth of our union with Christ. However, while recommending Norman's books, in no way do I make a claim to

be somehow interpretive of Norman Grubb or to be representing him or his "teaching" in any way. I hope only in some very small fashion to convey a little, tiny portion of the all-encompassing light that I received from God through Norman Grubb. Many of his books are still in print, and may be ordered by visiting www.christasus.com or www.normangrubb.com. I cannot also fail to mention some of the multitude of others who have contributed in major ways to my life and understanding: especially writers Thomas Merton, Jacob Boehme, Walter Lanyon, William Law, Robert Pirsig and John Irving, (and a thousand more), as well as all my friends, co-conspirators, lovers, "Bible pen pals" and everybody in between -- Janis Pruitt (my wife) and our three "grown" children (and spouses) and four grandchildren, John and Linda Bunting, Dan Stone, Ray and Marian Sandbek, Wade and Harriet Wearren, Alex Cohen, Scott and Sylvia Pearce, Brian and Tandy Coatney, Billy and Mimi Anderson, DeeDee Winter, John Collings, Tony and Bette Ketcham, Jack and Alice Corcoran and many many others. I am eternally grateful to them all, mentioned and unmentioned.

About the Author

Fred Pruitt lives with his wife, Janis, in Louisville, Kentucky. They are the parents of three, and grandparents of four. Fred started writing on the subject of union with Christ in the 1980s, his articles appearing in various magazines. Hearts of Flesh is his first full-length book.

18055599R00145

Made in the USA
Lexington, KY
12 October 2012